REMOTE PERFORMANCES IN NATURE AND ARCHITECTURE

Remote Performances in Nature and Architecture

Edited by

Bruce Gilchrist and Jo Joelson
London Fieldworks, UK

and

Tracey Warr
Oxford Brookes University, UK

Co-published with the Live Art Development Agency

© Bruce Gilchrist, Jo Joelson and Tracey Warr 2015
All texts © The Authors

All rights reserved. No part of this publication may be reproduced, stored in a retrieval system or transmitted in any form or by any means, electronic, mechanical, photocopying, recording or otherwise without the prior permission of the publisher.

Bruce Gilchrist, Jo Joelson and Tracey Warr have asserted their right under the Copyright, Designs and Patents Act, 1988, to be identified as the editors of this work.

Published by
Ashgate Publishing Limited
Wey Court East
Union Road
Farnham
Surrey, GU9 7PT
England

Ashgate Publishing Company
110 Cherry Street
Suite 3-1
Burlington, VT 05401-3818
USA

www.ashgate.com

Co-published by
Live Art Development Agency
The White Building
Unit 7, Queen's Yard
White Post Lane
London, E9 5EN
England

www.thisisLiveArt.co.uk

British Library Cataloguing in Publication Data
A catalogue record for this book is available from the British Library.

The Library of Congress has catalogued the printed edition as follows:
Remote performances in nature and architecture / Edited by Bruce Gilchrist, Jo Joelson and Tracey Warr.
   pages cm
 Includes bibliographical references and index.
  ISBN 978-1-4724-5393-8 (hardback) -- ISBN 978-1-4724-5391-4 (ebook) -- ISBN 978-1-4724-5392-1 (epub) 1. Human ecology in art. 2. Nature (Aesthetics) 3. Art, Modern--21st century--Themes, motives. 4. London Fieldworks. I. Gilchrist, Bruce, 1959- editor. II. Joelson, Jo, 1969- editor. III. Warr, Tracey, editor.
 N8217.E28R46 2015
 709.411'56--dc23

2015011144

ISBN: 978-1-4724-5391-4 (hbk)
ISBN: 978-1-4724-5392-1 (ebk – PDF)
ISBN: 978-1-4724-5393-8 (ebk – ePUB)

Printed in the United Kingdom by Henry Ling Limited, at the Dorset Press, Dorchester, DT1 1HD

Contents

List of Figures	*vii*
List of Plates	*ix*
Notes on Contributors	*xiii*
Acknowledgements	*xxi*

Introduction
Jo Joelson
1

A Survey of the Terrain
Francis McKee
11

Kelpies, Banshees and Pibrochs Heard in these Parts
Geoff Sample
15

Like Like
Michael Pedersen
21

Selections from The Hut Book
Alec Finlay
25

From a Train
Goodiepal
33

The Sound of Lochaber
London Fieldworks and Mark Vernon
37

Geo Graphy
Tracey Warr
43

There's a Monster in the Nest-box *Clair Chinnery*	55
In Search of Silence *Lisa O'Brien*	63
Composing with Place *Kirsteen Davidson Kelly*	69
A Sense of Distance *Lee Patterson*	73
Notes for a Video *Benedict Drew*	77
The Contemporary Remote *Bruce Gilchrist*	83
Second Sketch for Ascent and Descent *Ed Baxter*	91
Euphonium at Sea *Sarah Kenchington*	101
Notes After a Week of Wandering *Bram Thomas Arnold*	105
Echo. Genius Loci *Ruth Barker*	113
Into *Outlandia* *Johny Brown*	129
High-Lands *Tony White*	141
Endnotes on Remoteness *Clair Chinnery* *Lisa O'Brien* *Bram Thomas Arnold*	151
Further Resources	*157*
Index	*159*

List of Figures

Figure 1	Boardwalk to *Outlandia*, 2010	1
Figure 2	*Field sketch*, 2007	3
Figure 3	*Outlandia* drawing, 2007	3
Figure 4	*Outlandia*, 2010	4
Figure 5	*Outlandia* (interior view), 2010	5
Figure 6	*A Journey through the Great Glen to the Library of* Outlandia, hand-drawn map, 2010	6
Figure 7	*Bibliotheque Outlandia*, installation, 2010	7
Figure 8	*Outlandia* with satellite dish, 2014	8
Figure 9	Peter Lanceley with tooway satellite, 2014	9
Figure 10	*View of Ben Nevis*, 2014	11
Figure 11	Geoff Sample, *Remote Performances* broadcast, 4 August 2014	15
Figure 12	Loch Eil, 2014	21
Figure 13	*Circle Poem (for* Outlandia*)*, 2010	25
Figure 14	*Sweeney's Bothy*, Isle of Eigg (Alec Finlay and The Bothy Project), 2014	26
Figure 15	*Inshriach Bothy*, Cairngorms, The Bothy Project, 2013	30
Figure 16	Goodiepal, *Remote Performances* broadcast, 9 August 2014	33
Figure 17	*A Message to the International Hacker Community*, handwritten note, 2014	35
Figure 18	Arisaig Highland Games, August 2014	37
Figure 19	Arriving at Lochailort Station, August 2014	43
Figure 20	Peter May, *A Generall Survey of the Town of Gordon'sburgh with the houses gardens and other lands contiguous there-to. The property of his Grace Allexr, Duke of Gordon*, 1753	44
Figure 21	*Boatswain's Call*, video still, 2013	55
Figure 22	*Generic Highland Hybrid Host 2*, timelapse sequence, 2014	60
Figure 23	*Generic Highland Hybrid Host 2*, composite photo, 2014	61

Figure 24	Lisa O'Brien, *Remote Performances* broadcast, August 2014	63
Figure 25	*Balgy Panorama left*, 297 x 210 mm, pencil on paper, 2014	65
Figure 26	*Torridon Forest, January*, 594 x 420 mm, watercolour and ink on watercolour paper, 2014	67
Figure 27	Upright Piano, Glen Nevis, 2014	69
Figure 28	*Composition 2*, extract, performed by Kirsteen Davidson Kelly in Glen Nevis, 2014	71
Figure 29	Charlie Menzies, *Glen Nevis improvisation*, 2014	72
Figure 30	Lee Patterson, fieldwork in upper Glen Nevis, August 2014	73
Figure 31	Benedict Drew, fieldwork, Roshven, video still, August 2014	77
Figure 32	London Fieldworks, *Polaria* fieldwork, Hold With Hope Peninsula, Northeast Greenland, 2001	83
Figure 33	Fixed 42 metre UHF parabolic antenna, Eiscat Svalbard Radar, Frontiers 8, 2004	88
Figure 34	Tam Dean Burn performing for Ed Baxter's *Second Sketch for Ascent and Descent*, video still, August 2014	91
Figure 35	'Plea for Action to End Carnage …', *Lochaber News*, 31 July 2014	94
Figure 36	Danger of Death, Glen Nevis, August 2014	95
Figure 37	Sarah Kenchington, Loch Ailort, August 2014	101
Figure 38	Sarah Kenchington, Sea Euphonium, Loch Ailort, August 2014	103
Figure 39	*Throwing Rocks at Trees*, performance still, *Remote Performances*, Glen Nevis, Scotland, August 2014	105
Figure 40	*Reading Particle Physics to a River*, performance still, *Remote Performances*, Glen Nevis, Scotland, August 2014	108
Figure 41	*Reading Poetry to a Rock*, performance still, *Remote Performances*, Glen Nevis, Scotland, August 2014	109
Figure 42	Ruth Barker in *Outlandia*, August 2014	113
Figure 43	Johny Brown MCing *Remote Performances*, August 2014	129
Figure 44	Uher reel to reel tape machine used in Johny Brown's live radio play *Into Outlandia*, August 2014	140
Figure 45	Tony White, *Remote Performances* broadcast, 6 August 2014	141
Figure 46	*Outlandia* with satellite dish, August 2014	154
Figure 47	View from *Outlandia*, Glen Nevis, August 2014	154
Figure 48	*Outlandia*, August 2014	155
Figure 49	Tam Dean Burn, Loch Ailort Inn, August 2014	155
Figure 50	Johny Brown and James Stephen Finn, Tradewinds, Corpach, August 2014	156
Figure 51	Left to right: Benedict Drew, Lee Patterson, Bruce Gilchrist, Tam Dean Burn, Johny Brown, James Stephen Finn, Corpach, August 2014	156

List of Plates

Cover:	*Reflections across Glen Nevis*, 2013
	Source: Courtesy of the artist, Katy Connor
Plate i	*Notes for a Video*, digital collage, 2014
	Source: Courtesy of the artist, Benedict Drew, and Matt's Gallery
Plate ii	*Notes for a Video*, digital collage, 2014
	Source: Courtesy of the artist, Benedict Drew, and Matt's Gallery
Plate iii	*Notes for a Video*, digital collage, 2014
	Source: Courtesy of the artist, Benedict Drew, and Matt's Gallery
Plate iv	*Notes for a Video*, digital collage, 2014
	Source: Courtesy of the artist, Benedict Drew, and Matt's Gallery
Plate v	*View from Outlandia*, 2014
	Source: Inga Tillere
Plate vi	*Outlandia*, 2013
	Source: Luke Allan
Plate vii	*Outlandia* (interior), 2010
	Source: London Fieldworks
Plate viii	*Outlandia*, 2010
	Source: London Fieldworks
Plate ix	*Outlandia* boardwalk, 2014
	Source: Inga Tillere
Plate x	Understory, 2014
	Source: Inga Tillere
Plate xi	Start of the *Outlandia* boardwalk, 2013
	Source: Luke Allan
Plate xii	Ingrid Henderson en route to *Outlandia*, 2014
	Source: London Fieldworks
Plate xiii	*Local Spot* broadcast: Ingrid Henderson, 5 August 2014
	Source: Inga Tillere

Plate xiv	*Local Spot* broadcast: Cèilidh Trailers, 4 August 2014 *Source*: Inga Tillere
Plate xv	*Local Spot* broadcast: Isabel Campbell and Ian McColl, 6 August 2014 *Source*: Inga Tillere
Plate xvi	*Local Spot* broadcast: John Hutchison, 8 August 2014 *Source*: Inga Tillere
Plate xvii	*Local Spot* broadcast: Alex Gillespie, 7 August 2014 *Source*: Inga Tillere
Plate xviii	*Local Spot* broadcast: Willie Anderson, 7 August 2014 *Source*: Inga Tillere
Plate xix	*Local Spot* broadcast: Emma Nicholson, 8 August 2014 *Source*: Inga Tillere
Plate xx	Sarah Nicol and John Ireland looking for Hairy Wood Ants, 2014 *Source*: London Fieldworks
Plate xxi	Lisa O'Brien, fieldwork in upper Glen Nevis with Peter Lanceley, August 2014 *Source*: London Fieldworks
Plate xxii	Mark Vernon field-recording at the Loch Eilde Mor hydroelectric generating station, Kinlochleven, July 2014 *Source*: London Fieldworks
Plate xxiii	Mark Vernon, *vox pop* at Cameron Square, Fort William, July 2014 *Source*: London Fieldworks
Plate xxiv	*Big Pipe*, Loch Ailort, August 2014 *Source*: Courtesy of the artist, Sarah Kenchington
Plate xxv	Sarah Kenchington, *Euphonium at Sea*, Loch Ailort, August 2014 *Source*: London Fieldworks
Plate xxvi	*Generic Highland Hybrid Host 1*, installation at Outlandia, 2013 *Source*: Courtesy of the artist, Clair Chinnery
Plate xxvii	Aftermath of Clair Chinnery, *Generic Highland Hybrid Host 2*, August 2014 *Source*: London Fieldworks
Plate xxviii	Clair Chinnery, *The Boatswain's Call*, video still, Glenuig, August 2014 *Source*: Courtesy of the artist, Clair Chinnery
Plate xxix	Bram Thomas Arnold, *Swearing An Oath To A Scottish Glen*, performance still, *Remote Performances*, Glen Nevis, Scotland, August 2014 *Source*: London Fieldworks
Plate xxx	*A Message to the International Hacker Community*, August 2014 *Source*: Courtesy of the artist, Goodiepal, and London Fieldworks
Plate xxxi	Goodiepal posting *A Message to the International Hacker Community*, August 2014 *Source*: Courtesy of the artist and London Fieldworks

Plate xxxii	Lee Patterson, field recording, upper Glen Nevis, August 2014
	Source: London Fieldworks
Plate xxxiii	Lee Patterson and Bruce Gilchrist, field recording, Loch Ailort, August 2014
	Source: Inga Tillere
Plate xxxiv	Ruth Barker, *Remote Performances* broadcast, 7 August 2014
	Source: Inga Tillere
Plate xxxv	Ken Cockburn and Alec Finlay, *Remote Performances* broadcast, 8 August 2014
	Source: Inga Tillere
Plate xxxvi	Resonance Radio Orchestra, *Remote Performances* broadcast, 9 August 2014
	Source: Inga Tillere
Plate xxxvii	Band of Holy Joy, *Remote Performances* broadcast, 8 August 2014
	Source: Inga Tillere
Plate xxxviii	Stuart Brisley, *Untitled Landscape* (verso), 31 cm x 53.5 cm, watercolour on card, 2 June 1953
	Source: Courtesy of the artist and Andy Keate
Plate xxxix	Stuart Brisley, *Untitled Landscape* (recto), 31 cm x 53.5 cm, watercolour on card, 2 June 1953
	Source: Courtesy of the artist and Andy Keate
Plate xl	Props for Band of Holy Joy, *Into Outlandia*, 8 August 2014
	Source: Inga Tillere

Notes on Contributors

Bram Thomas Arnold is an artist who started with walking and kept going: into performance, drawing, installation, bookbinding and writing. His transdisciplinary practice was instigated through studying Social Sculpture alongside Ecology under Shelley Sacks at Oxford Brookes University before undertaking an MA in Arts and Ecology at the now absent Dartington College of Arts. Alongside a transient upbringing, moving from Switzerland through Belgium and Holland into England and Wales, this interdisciplinary approach to study has manifested itself into a practice that is not restricted to traditional boundaries of mediums or modes of practice, a practice that is both Romantic and Conceptual in methods and outcomes. As an artist he has built a piece of road in a forest, carried 60 English novels to New York, learned to translate Lithuanian and set out to walk from his home in London to the place of his birth in St. Gallen, Switzerland. His ecologically minded practice has been exhibited broadly in the UK as well as abroad in exhibitions from New York to St. Petersburg. He is currently studying for a practice-based PhD at Falmouth University where his interests in performance, installation, autoethnography and transdisciplinary practice are being developed through a research project entitled *Walking Home: The path as transect in an 800 kilometre autoethnographic enquiry*. http://www.bramthomasarnold.com

Ruth Barker is a Glasgow based artist who works with text and performance. Her practice throws moments of the contemporary quotidian up against the accumulated echoes of humanity's oldest stories. Reflecting theoretical ideas of connectivity and finitude, Barker discovers ancient myths in her unconscious associations and personal autobiography. Barker's performance poems are hypnotic, ritualised events that are layered in intensity. Spanning epic durations, her words have a concentrated focus that is magical, claustrophobic, meditative and cathartic. Recent projects include performance commissions for Glasgow Women's Library, Camden Arts Centre (London), Sils Projects (Rotterdam), Glasgow

International festival of Visual Art; Cartel Gallery, (London); ReMap festival (Athens); the Centre for Interdisciplinary Artefact Studies (Newcastle); and Machon Hamayim (Tel Aviv).
http://www.ruthbarker.com

Ed Baxter is the CEO of Resonance104.4fm; was BASCA Composer of the Year (Sonic Arts) 2013; nominated Station Programmer of the Year, Sony Radio Academy Awards 2010; featured in the *Independent on Sunday*'s Happy List 2009; runner up, PRSF New Music Award 2008; and is an Associate Lecturer, London College of Communication (Sound Arts and Design). Ed was awarded a PhD in 1987 and was a co-editor of *The Works Of Thomas De Quincey*. He has also been a curator, concert and tour organiser, journalist, book seller, and installation artist. He formed the Resonance Radio Orchestra with Chris Weaver in 2004 as a floating pool for radiophonic experimentation, the various incarnations of which have included *i.a.* Fari Bradley, Tam Dean Burn, Luke Fowler, John Paul Jones, Taigen Kawabe, Peter Lanceley, Robin Warren and Veryan Weston.
https://resonanceradioorchestra.wordpress.com

Johny Brown leads the Band of Holy Joy and oversees a weekly Friday night radio show on Resonance 104.4fm called *BAD PUNK*. He has written drama for both stage and radio. His plays have been presented at venues including The Citizen's Glasgow, the Traverse Edinburgh, and the Theatre D'Ville in Paris.
http://www.bandofholyjoy.co.uk

Clair Chinnery is an artist who lives and works in Oxford, UK where she is a Senior Lecturer in Fine Art at Oxford Brookes University. Her recent practice and projects place emphases on metaphors of colonial history and narratives of human migration. Her interest lies at the intersection of evolutionary and non-evolutionary animal behaviour juxtaposed with an exploration of the human impulse to collect, order and archive through museums and other cultural formations. Notably, her works explore and illuminate the institutional conventions of how nature and culture are historicised and 'packaged' to the public. They are concerned with what accumulations, and re-presentations of natural and cultural artefacts (through collections, archives and museums) tell us about the colonising impulses of 'human animals', how such impulses have parallels in the natural world, and how in making metaphorical links/crossovers and/juxtapositions between the two, new ways of thinking about our place and roles in the contemporary world emerge. Parts of this process can be found in key works where she uses 'hybridity' as a means, mimicry as an anthropomorphic device, and 'absence' and 'removal' as a narrative tool, to reflect both colonial and institutional practices and conventions of belonging and non-belonging. She exhibits her work nationally and internationally in galleries and other contexts, appropriate to location (for example, in historic civic buildings, museum collections of Natural History and more remote sites). Works from her project *Cuculus Prospectus* have been exhibited at Beldam Gallery, Brunel University; Waterfront Gallery, UCS, Ipswich; Ipswich Museum; Cornerstone Arts,

Oxfordshire; Curious Matter, NJ, USA; and have also been sited in the civic spaces of Oxford Town Hall.
https://wiki.brookes.ac.uk/display/arp/Clair+Chinnery

Kirsteen Davidson Kelly is a pianist, music educator and researcher based in South West Scotland. She co-founded the innovative ensemble Piano Circus where she stayed for thirteen years, commissioning and performing works by composers such as Julia Wolfe, David Lang, Graham Fitkin and Nikki Yeoh, and appearing at major venues internationally. Kirsteen has recorded extensively for Decca and other labels, including classic works by Steve Reich, Terry Riley, Graham Fitkin and Stravinsky. In 2002 she co-produced Piano Circus's critically acclaimed CD *Transmission*. Current projects include the two piano duo *KDKDK* with pianist Katharine Durran, performing some of the most exuberant and virtuosic twentieth and twenty-first century music for two pianos, regular performances of work by Max Richter, and a performance, installation and recording project with Edinburgh-based composer Vroni Holzmann. Kirsteen has collaborated with dancers, physical theatre practitioners, visual artists, filmmakers, composers and musicians – both as a performer and through creative education projects with diverse communities internationally. In 2014 she completed a PhD that explored ways in which musicians imagine music during preparation for performance, and which included a brain imaging (fMRI) study of expert pianists.
http://www.researchgate.net/profile/Kirsteen_Davidson-kelly

Benedict Drew (born 1977) works across video, sculpture, music and their associated technologies. He is represented by Matt's Gallery, London. Recent solo exhibitions include: *Heads May Roll*, Matt's Gallery, London; *The Persuaders*', Adelaide Festival, SASA Gallery Adelaide, Australia; *Zero Hour Petrified*, Ilam Campus Gallery, School of Fine Arts University of Canterbury, New Zealand (all 2014); *The Onesie Cycle,* Rhubarba, Edinburgh; *Now Thing*, Whitstable Biennale; *This Is Feedback*, Outpost, Norwich; *Gliss*, Cell Project Space; and *The Persuaders*, Circa Site / AV Festival, Newcastle.
http://www.benedictdrew.com

Alec Finlay is an artist and poet, living in Edinburgh,working across a wide range of media and forms – including text, sculpture, mapping, books, print-works, and new technology – Finlay's work considers how we as a culture, or cultures, relate to landscape and ecology. His work has been exhibited at Tate, BALTIC, and the Sydney Biennale, and was shortlisted for the 2010 Northern Art Prize and the 2012 Artistic Landmarks in Contemporary Experience Award. Recent journey and mapping projects include *The Road North* (2010–11), *Out of Books* (2012–14), both with Ken Cockburn, and *A Company of Mountains* (2012). His work is often collaborative, for example working with The Bothy Project to create Sweeney's Bothy, a pioneering artist residency space on the Isle of Eigg. Finlay's other innovative 'shelters' include his Woodland Platform at the hidden gardens in Glasgow, the Renga Platform at The Garden Station, Hexham, and most recently a memorial 'Taigh', at the Royal

Botanic Garden Edinburgh. Recent books include *Global Oracle* (2014), *a-ga: on mountains* (2014), *Taigh: a wilding garden* (2014) and *The Road North* (2014). He is represented by Ingleby Gallery and blogs at:
www.alecfinlay.com

Bruce Gilchrist – see London Fieldworks.

Goodiepal, or **Gæoudji Sygnok** (Parl Kristian Bjørn Vester), is a Faroese/Danish musician, composer, and writer. His work often involves lectures and performances on the future of computer music, his own compositional practices and resonance computing, and his tours have included 150 universities internationally. From 2004 to 2008 he was head of the electronic music department and teacher at DIEM (Danish Institute for Electro-acoustic Music) at the Royal Academy of Music in Aarhus, Denmark. He is the author of two books, *Radical Computer Music and Fantastisk Mediemanipulation* (2009) and *El Camino Del Hardcore – Rejsen Til Nordens Indre* (2012). Goodiepal is also known for travelling over very long distances only using his home-made electricity-producing bike, *Kommunal Klon Komputer 2*, and for production of his own electricity to power electronic music equipment with dynamos. In 2014, he sold the bike to the National Gallery of Denmark, and it is now on display. A new bike is in the making, Kommunal Klon Komputer 9. His work *Narc Beacon* was awarded an honourable mention at the Ars Electronica (2002). He was commissioned to create a sound piece representing Norway, Denmark, Sweden, Iceland and Greenland at the World Expo 2005 in Aichi, Japan. *Mort Aux Vaches Ekstra Extra* was presented at the 5th Berlin Biennale for Contemporary Art, 2008. He received a first class merit certificate as StoryTellerScotland in 2008. He is now officially allowed to call himself a *Master Storyteller* of the highest accord in the UK. He received the Danish Heinrich Prize at Den Grå Hal, Christiania in 2010 for his contestation with the Royal Academy of Music.
http://vimeo.com/105115205
https://vimeo.com/11152592

Jo Joelson – see London Fieldworks.

Sarah Kenchington has been building and adapting musical instruments for the past 10 years. All of her instruments are human powered, mechanically assisted, acoustic devices. Some are designed to be played in a conventional sense, like her pedal powered double-ended hurdy gurdy/banjo. Others are designed to compose the music, like the *Bell Tower*: a pyramid structure that distributes balls in a mathematical pattern. Her *Flutterbox*, a mechanical sequencer, generates rhythmic loops, or colour coded musical notation. In her performances Kenchington plays a semi-mechanical, pedal and pump powered orchestra, involving many of her instruments at the same time. She has performed internationally at experimental music festivals including *Suoni Per Il Popolo*, Montreal (2012), and *Tectonics*, Glasgow (2014) and also as part of theatre and film projects including *Circus Invisible*

(2011) and *Dummy Jim* (2008). Another strand of her work has been creating large scale musical installations to be played by the public. These include: *Sound House* for the Museum of Modern Art in Oxford (2009), an instrument made from a council house; *Sound Dome* for the Tramway in Glasgow (2010), a giant inside out string instrument, played from inside the sound box; and *Wind Pipes*, for the Edinburgh Art Festival (2013), a hand pumped pipe organ designed to be played by twelve people at once. Kenchington is currently collaborating with Icelandic contemporary orchestral music collective SLATUR, to create machines that blur the boundary between instrument, composer and conductor, for a performance in Reykjavik in 2015.

London Fieldworks (LFW) is an interdisciplinary and collaborative arts practice formed in 2000 by artists Bruce Gilchrist and Jo Joelson, based in east London. A notion of ecology as a complex inter-working of social, natural, and technological worlds informs their projects across social engagement, installation, and moving image to situate works both in the gallery and in the landscape. Signature works often attend to place and to habitat, building and sustaining interdisciplinary architectures and structures of engagement; investigating the meeting points of culture and nature through constructed interventions and installations. Recent exhibitions include Microwave International New Media Arts Festival, Hong Kong; Tropixel Festival, Ubatuba, Brazil; Bio-Fiction, Vienna; Trafo Gallery, Budapest; Tranzit. ro, Bucharest; The Negligent Eye, Bluecoat Gallery, Liverpool; Sprengel Museum, Hannover. Their work has been featured in a number of publications including, *On Not Knowing: How Artists Think* (Black Dog, 2013); *Null Object: Gustav Metzger Thinks About Nothing* (Black Dog, 2012); *Far Field* (Intellect Books, 2011); *Searching for Art's New Publics* (Intellect Books, 2010); *ART+SCIENCE NOW: A Visual Survey of Artists Working at the Frontiers of Science and Technology* (Thames and Hudson, 2010); *Beyond Architecture: Imaginative Buildings and Fictional Cities* (Gestalten, 2009). Supported by the British Council, Arts Council England, National Endowment for the Arts (USA) and Calouste Gulbenkian Foundation among others, LFW projects have received awards from The Arts Foundation; Ars Electronica, Linz; VIDA, Art and Artificial Life, Madrid and London Short Film Festival (Best Experimental Short 2014*)*.
http://www.londonfieldworks.com

Francis McKee is the director of the Centre for Contemporary Arts in Glasgow and a research fellow at The Glasgow School of Art. His research interests include the exploration of open source theory as a potential economic model within the arts, the role of the archive in contemporary art, and modes of curatorial practice. He presented the exhibition and symposium, *Agile Process: A New Economy for Digital Arts in Scotland*. Since 2011 he has been lead researcher in the AHRC funded project, *The Glasgow Miracle*, centring on the archiving of forty years material from the Third Eye Centre and the CCA. From 2005 to 2008 he was curator of *Glasgow International Festival of Contemporary Visual Art*. He has curated many exhibitions including *This Peaceful War*,

The Jumex Collection for the first *Glasgow International* in 2005; *Zenomap* (together with Kay Pallister), the presentation of new work from Scotland for the *Venice Biennale* in 2003; and he was one of the invited curators for the *Lyon Biennale* in 2007. Previously he worked as a historian of medicine for the Wellcome Trust and as Head of Programme at CCA. For the past fifteen years he has written extensively on the work of artists such as Christine Borland, Willie Docherty, Ross Sinclair, Douglas Gordon, Matthew Barney, Simon Starling, Catherine Yass, Joao Penalva, Kathy Prendergast and Pipilotti Rist. A recent collection of essays has been published and he was one of seven writers to collaborate on a sci-fi novel entitled *Philip*.
http://francismckee.net

Lisa O'Brien is an interdisciplinary artist using video, sound, photography and drawing to explore and research often remote places, changing weather conditions and how they impact on us. She has a phenomenological approach using different media to capture her personal experience of different spaces and events and she is also interested in how we experience duration and subsequent memory of a place or event. Her work has been exhibited nationally and internationally including touring with New Media Scotland and also JICPB Cube Gallery – an initiative that made connections with galleries in remote locations in Scotland, Japan, Denmark and France. More recently she has focused on the remote landscape of North West Scotland where she has lived for the last 10 years and where she walks and draws in the local woods and forest.
http://www.lisaobrien.co.uk
http://www.axisweb.org/features/profile/open-frequency/lisa-obrien-2006/

Lee Patterson is an artist who, through acts of listening with both aided and naked ears, attempts to understand elements of his surroundings and culture by the sounds found therein. The accompanying use of sound recording as a method to educate his perception of things, has led to a variety of projects ranging across environmental sound, improvised music, film soundtrack, radio and installation. Whether working live with amplification – as both a form of manipulation and a mode of enquiry, or recording within an environment, he has pioneered a range of devices and methods that produce or uncover complex sound in unexpected places. From rock chalk to burning nuts, from bridges to aquatic plants, he eavesdrops upon the sounds emitted by organisms and objects otherwise considered mute. Past and present collaborators include Mika Vainio, Vanessa Rossetto, David Toop, Rhodri Davies and John Butcher, Greg Pope, Luke Fowler, Lucio Capece, Rie Nakajima, Angharad Davies, Keith Rowe, John Tilbury, Xavier Charles and Tetsuya Umeda. His works have appeared on UK TV, BBC Radios 3, 4 and 6, Resonance104.4fm and on radio stations worldwide.

Michael Pedersen is a poet, playwright and *animateur* with an electric reputation. He has collaborated with artists, musicians and film-makers and has two successful chapbooks and a debut collection (*Play With Me* published by Polygon) under his belt. He writes lyrics for bands and co-runs/co-founded the Neu! Reekie! arts

collective and record label. Michael was named a 'Canongate Future 40' and was recently awarded the John Mather Trust Rising Star of Literate Award. Stephen Fry comments: 'Michael's poems are so physical you can almost touch the images in them. Fabulously sensual and alive. I adore poetry like this'. Irvine Welsh remarks: 'If you like poetry that is cool, smart, hilarious and quirky and can just suddenly rip your heart out, Michael Pedersen is your man'.
http://www.birlinn.co.uk/Play-With-Me.html

Geoff Sample specialises in recording birds and natural soundscapes as fine art and documentary. He combines a musician's ear with an extensive knowledge of bioacoustic science and the cultural history of hearing music in nature. For 20 years he has released albums in this field through the Wildsong label. His natural history work includes seven sound guides to wildlife (book and CDs), published by HarperCollins and numerous commissions from other publishers and conservation organisations. His recordings, composition and insight are regularly called upon by musicians, sound designers, BBC radio, TV and feature films. Art projects and collaborations have ranged from the multi-screen installation *Dawn Chorus* with Marcus Coates (2007), the multi-channel outdoor audio installation *Natural Soundscapes of Britain* (2011) at the Southbank, London, to the exploratory local acoustic ecology project *Sounding Out Bedlington* (2005) and *Where We Belong* (2015). Recent collaborations exploring sound, music and landscape have included Hanna Tuulikki's *Away with the Birds* and Lucy Stevens's *Representing Birdsong*. Sample's practice uses sound and words, framing distance, condensing time and wandering the borders of nature-culture, to connect with the mythogenic landscapes of our collective psyche.
http://geoffsample.com

Mark Vernon is a sound artist and radio producer based in Glasgow. He has produced programmes internationally for radio stations including Wave Farm, Kunstradio, RADIA, Resonance 104.4fm, CKUT, VPRO and BBC Radio 4. He has also been involved in the creation of UK art radio projects: *Radiophrenia, Hairwaves, Radio Tuesday* and *Nowhere Island Radio*. He records and performs both solo and in various collaborative music projects with record releases on Staalplaat, Ultra Eczema, Entr'acte, Staubgold and Gagarin Records. Together with Monica Brown he runs Lights Out Listening Group, a monthly listening event focused on creative uses of sound and radio that takes place in complete darkness.
http://www.meagreresource.com
https://soundcloud.com/markvernon
https://soundcloud.com/vernonandburns/
http://lightsoutlisteninggroup.wordpress.com/

Tracey Warr writes fiction and non-fiction. She has published two medieval novels, *Almodis* (Impress Books, 2011) and *The Viking Hostage* (Impress Books, 2014). *Almodis* was shortlisted for the Impress Prize for New Writing and for the Rome Film Festival Book Initiative. She is working on a new novel, supported by a Literature Wales Writer's Bursary, set in south west Wales in the 12th and 23rd centuries, and contemplating a future of climate change and its environmental and social impacts. She is also working on a biography, entitled *Three Female Lords*, about three noblewomen in southern France and northern Spain in the 11th century. Her publications on contemporary artists include *A Study Room Guide to Remoteness* (LADA, 2014), *Setting the Fell on Fire* (Editions North, 2009), *The Artist's Body* (Phaidon, 2000) and essays in *Women, the Arts and Globalization* (Manchester University Press, 2013), *Intimacy Across Visceral and Digital Performance* (Palgrave Macmillan, 2012), *Sensualities/Textualities and Technologies: Writings of the Body in 21st Century Performance* (Palgrave Macmillan, 2010), *Panic Attack!: Art in the Punk Years* (Merrell, 2007), *Art, Lies & Videotape* (Tate, 2003), *Marcus Coates* (Grizedale, 2002) and *London Fieldworks: Syzygy/Polaria* (Black Dog, 2002), She also writes book reviews for *Times Higher Education*, *New Welsh Review* and *Historical Novels Review*. She is currently a commissioned writer in the *Frontiers in Retreat* project working with Jutempus in Lithuania and undertaking writer's residencies at Centre d'Art i Natura, Farrera, Spain and HIAP, Helsinki, Finland. http://traceywarrwriting.com

Tony White is the author of novels including *Shackleton's Man Goes South* (Science Museum) and *Foxy-T* (Faber and Faber), the non-fiction work *Another Fool in the Balkans* (Cadogan) and numerous short stories. He has edited and co-edited the short story anthologies *Britpulp* (Sceptre) and – with Matt Thorne and Borivoj Radakovic – *Croatian Nights* (Serpent's Tail). Other recent works include *Missorts*, a permanent GPS-triggered sound-work for Bristol, and an accompanying novella *Missorts Volume II* (Situations). His novella *Dicky Star and the Garden Rule* (Forma) was commissioned alongside works by the artists Jane and Louise Wilson to mark the twenty-fifth anniversary of the Chernobyl disaster. A frequent writer about art, White has edited and published the artists' book imprint Piece of Paper Press since 1994. He was formerly writer in residence at the Science Museum and Leverhulme Trust writer in residence at UCL School of Slavonic and East European Studies. At the time of writing he was Creative Entrepreneur in Residence and a visiting research fellow at King's College, London. http://pieceofpaperpress.com/

Acknowledgements

Thanks to our editor at Ashgate, Valerie Rose, for guiding us so well through the publication process, and to our meticulous production editor, Gillian Steadman.

Remote Performances in Nature and Architecture has been financially supported by Arts Council England, Nevis Landscape Partnership, Oxford Brookes University and Live Art Development Agency.

Special thanks to John O'Kane, formerly of The Highland Council, for his commitment and advocacy throughout the development of Outlandia; to Malcolm Fraser and Niall Jacobson for their adventurous architectural approach and to Norman Clark, Ali Berardelli and Alex and Mary Gillespie, whose many contributions and ongoing support locally is so appreciated. Thank you to the Forestry Commission Scotland for their long-term partnership and project assistance. Thanks to Tristan Semple whose recognition of *Outlandia* has helped to foster a new alliance with the Nevis Landscape Partnership and to Freja MacDougall for continuing to support and drive this forwards.

Our thanks to Lois Keidan, Alex Eisenberg and the rest of the team at Live Art Development Agency, (Katy Baird, Aaron Wright and C.J. Mitchell) for publishing support, *Remote Performances* blogpost and listening post hosting. Thanks also to Caithness Horizons and Edinburgh Art Festival 2014 for listening post/project hosting.

We are grateful to Alison Austin, Sorcha Carey, Marcus Coates, Barry Esson, Alice Ladenburg and Paul Whitty for their helpful contributions with contacts and connections during the early development stages of *Remote Performances*.

Respect and gratitude to Resonance104.4fm for co-production of *Remote Performances* and to the team of Ed Baxter, Peter Lanceley, Sarah Nicol and Michael Umney for leading on production and managing the many technical challenges posed by the project.

Huge thanks to Johny Brown and Tam Dean Burn who were the inimitable radio MCs and to Inga Tillere for her dedicated approach to the documentation of *Remote Performances* and for allowing us to share her photographs in this book. Thanks also go to all the photographers whose images appear in the book, including Anthony Oliver and Jo Outram who were the documentors for *Polaria*.

We are indebted to all the writers, artists, participants and collaborators whose unique contributions, insights and experiences have created such a rich and eclectic project and publication. Artist collaborators include Ewen Campbell, Ziggy Campbell, Ken Cockburn, Lorna Finlayson, James Stephen Finn, Francis and Olivia Frascina, Miriam Iorwerth and Charlie Menzies. Local spot participants included: Willy Anderson, Isabel Campbell MBE, Céilidh Trailers, Laura Davies, Caitrin Edmond, Alex Gillespie, Ingrid Henderson, John Hutchison MBE, John Ireland, Liam Maclean, Stephanie MacKenna, Ian McColl, Emma Nicholson, and Alex Du Toit. Contributors to *Sound of Lochaber* programmes included: Lila Berardelli, Paolo Berardelli, Isabel Campbell, Malcolm Fraser, Ingrid Henderson, Jetson Joelson Gilchrist, Charlie MacFarlane, Joe O'Connell, Lochaber Strathspey and Reel Society, Room 13.

Thanks to Lochaber Archive Centre, Karen Haggerty at Glen Nevis Visitor Centre, Lochaber College, BOC, Loch Ness Pianos, New Start Highland and to Craig Statham at National Library of Scotland.

Thank you to Jennie and David Erdal, Helen Lucas and Malcolm Fraser whose homes provided a special artist base and to Patricia Smith who catered and supported tremendously.

And finally thank you to the *Outlandia* Steering Group in Fort William who provide essential support and advice: Ali Berardelli, Richard Bracken, Norman Clark, Pamela Conacher, Lorna Finlayson, Helen Lucas, Freja MacDougall, Craig Miller, Tristan Semple, Peter Varley, Tracey Warr, Ruari Watt.

Introduction

Jo Joelson

Fig. 1 Boardwalk to *Outlandia*, 2010
Source: Kristian Buus

In early 2005 London Fieldworks was exhibiting a video and sound installation at the Nevis Centre in Fort William as part of the Mountain Film Festival. Local artists, historians, musicians, walkers, mountain climbers and rescue team members had worked with us to make the film (on Ben Nevis and Haldde Mountain in Northern Norway) and many more were involved in the civic twinning ceremony that formed a major part of the *Little Earth* project (Gilchrist and Joelson, 2005). It drew inspiration from the scientific history of Ben Nevis and Haldde Mountain, their summit observatories and the work of scientists, C.T.R. Wilson, and Kristian Birkeland who were stationed there in the 1890s. As we manned the installation at the Nevis Centre we got into conversation with many local people who expressed a need for more dedicated contemporary arts facilities and opportunities in the region.

Following the *Little Earth* project the Highland Council invited us to propose a public artwork to celebrate the Year of Highland Culture 2007. Having identified a lack of studio provision for local artists and opportunities for engagement with contemporary artists from outside the area, we started to explore the potential of creating a lasting legacy beyond 2007. We focused our attention on the Nevis landscape and its complex ecology combining human population, industry, heritage and natural environment. Home to Britain's highest mountain and the region branded the Outdoor Capital of the UK, Glen Nevis has been described as one of the most iconic living landscapes in Britain, with abundant natural history, archaeological sites including medieval earthworks, burial grounds, charcoal burners' platforms. Whilst much of Glen Nevis has one or more official designations of natural, historic and scientific interest and European importance, the ecology is under pressure from tens of thousands of visitors each year. There is a dichotomy within the landscape to function as an area of outstanding natural beauty as well as a resource for society's raw materials – a schism common to many rural communities.

Inspired by childhood dens, wildlife hides and bothies, we imagined a fieldstation for use by artists: local, national, international; a meeting place, a hideout, a shelter, a studio, a cabin in the forest, a platform for artists to be in residence, and for others to stumble across and wonder about its contents. We wanted the space to encourage creative interaction between artists and the land, its history and its people; to be off-grid, a space to disconnect, a sustainable sculpture, a contribution to contemporary arts development in Lochaber.

Between 2005 and 2010 there were multilayered investigations, dialogue and creative workings; we were engaged in complex negotiations that involved collaborators, partners, landowners, community and the local authority. Funding was sought, architects and engineers appointed (Malcolm Fraser Architects and Buro Happold Engineers), planning applications were made and withdrawn. Our proposal was controversial. The local media reported on the project with articles headlined: 'Culture year "tree houses" for artists cause row in glen'; 'Council's root and branch approach to tree houses'; 'Bark Raving Mad'. A new site was found, funding was received, some funding applications rejected; the project was scaled down, temporary planning permission was given, a contractor employed and in 2010, five long years after its inception, *Outlandia* was completed (*Outlandia* blog).

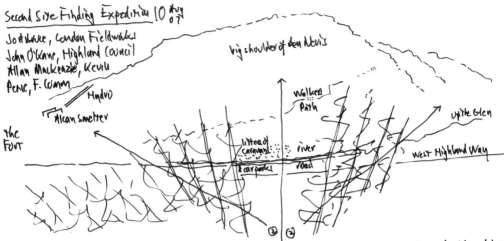

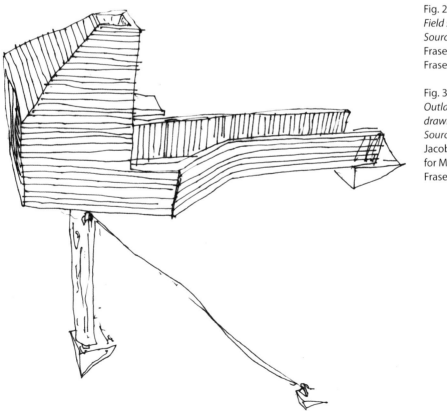

Fig. 2 (above)
Field sketch, 2007
Source: Malcolm Fraser for Malcolm Fraser Architects

Fig. 3 (left)
Outlandia drawing, 2007
Source: Niall Jacobson for Malcolm Fraser Architects

Fig. 4   Outlandia, 2010
Source: London Fieldworks

The fieldstation – a simple wooden cabin – sits on a platform supported from below by a tree and extending out from the 45-degree slope by a bridge, overlooking the Glen and facing Meall an t-Suidhe, and the western and southern flanks of Ben Nevis. The bridge transforms into a staircase to negotiate the steep incline, and for a quarter of a mile a specially constructed boardwalk traverses the dimly lit, boggy terrain (see Plates v–xi). The boardwalk eventually intersects

Fig. 5 *Outlandia* (interior view), 2010
Source: London Fieldworks

the Peat Track, a steep connection between Cow Hill and the final stretch of the West Highland Way below. Traditionally crofters grazed their cattle on the hill and used the track to bring peat cuttings down from the top, but hill-walking tourists attracted by the area's reputation as the 'Outdoor Capital of the UK' can now be found climbing up and down it. Curious walkers often journey down the boardwalk to encounter either an artist working in the cabin or a securely closed door. Its build was challenging: the site, on Forestry Commission land, is an extreme slope amongst a larch plantation some way off the beaten track and accessible only by foot. Part of its construction was low-impact, making use of material from the site and part high-impact, with a helicopter used to land concrete for the foundations. Architect Malcolm Fraser reflected on the construction process as 'part-joinery, part-forestry and part-mountain rescue' (Fraser, 2011), and local contractor, Norman Clark, a former downhill ski champion, usefully combined all three. Dave John and the Environmental Conservation Group at Lochaber College built the boardwalk through the forest to join the peat track near the summit of Cow Hill. Both the Peat Track and *Outlandia* boardwalk are used by Geocache hunters, an outdoor recreational activity originally referred to as GPS stash hunting or gpsstashing. Instigated by someone unknown to us, *Outlandia* has been designated a Geocache GPS coordinate, which locates a small, otherwise hidden, waterproof canister with logbook, pencil and trading items inside. Underpinning the *Outlandia* project, as a transformative creative potentiality is a diverse, attenuated alliance with adventure tourism and niche outdoor recreational activity.

The second chapter of *Outlandia* began in autumn 2010 with its public unveiling and launch, an event organised to coincide with the Great Glen Artists Airshow presented by Arts Catalyst in association with HICA (The Highland Institute of Contemporary Art). Artist Adam Dant created the inaugural installation at *Outlandia*, transforming the interior into a *trompe l'oeil* library in the style of the Scottish Enlightenment, the *Bibliotheque Outlandia*. Dant complemented this work with an aerial map *A Journey Through the Great Glen to the Library of Outlandia* which revealed unusual and hidden aspects during a perambulatory bus tour that set out from HICA to *Outlandia*. Since its launch *Outlandia* has hosted dozens of residencies for local, national and international artists and maintains a presence via on-line media, social networks, word of mouth and chance encounters via its various intersections.

Fig. 6 *A Journey through the Great Glen to the Library of* Outlandia, hand-drawn map, 2010 Source: Courtesy of the artist, Adam Dant and London Fieldworks

The *Remote Performances* project began as a publication idea conceived with Tracey Warr, with a focus on artist fieldwork and the way that being in the field permeates practice and output. The idea grew to embrace a range of media in dialogue with Johny Brown (musician, writer, DJ), Tam Dean Burn (actor and musician), Ed Baxter (Co-founder and CEO of Resonance 104.4fm) and Lois Keidan (Director of Live Art Development Agency).

Remote Performances took place in August 2014 when Outlandia was turned into a temporary radio station by the Resonance 104.4fm team comprising Ed Baxter, Peter Lanceley, Sarah Nicol, and Michael Umney (see *Remote Performances blog* including links to archived audio files of the broadcasts). *Outlandia*'s remote and

Fig. 7 *Bibliotheque Outlandia*, installation, 2010
Source: Courtesy of the artist, Adam Dant and London Fieldworks

off-grid location makes it a distinctive place to transmit from. Without connection to the National Grid there was the challenge of getting a temporary power supply to *Outlandia* to support the satellite broadcasting equipment. Traditional generators, which rely on diesel or petrol combustion engines, are noisy and this would interfere with the quality of the sound recordings. After the recce Resonance approached BOC to sponsor the project with their latest hydrogen generators. At 45 decibels, the Hymera portable generator proved to be extremely quiet and producing water as the only by-product it was also an environmentally friendly option.

The week-long series of radio broadcasts was co-produced by London Fieldworks and Resonance 104.4fm and included performances by 20 commissioned artists and interviews and performances by Lochaber residents and the local Nevis community. The MC-ing role was shared between Tam Dean Burn and Johny Brown who as well as being involved as artists, took turns to introduce each programme and interview the artists and performers. A total of 36 individual programmes were made and broadcast including a number of new artist collaborations that developed in the field; a series of programmes titled *The Sound of Lochaber* made by Mark Vernon, Bruce Gilchrist and Jo Joelson with local residents; and a 60 minute daily *Local Spot* (see Plates xiii–xix) which invited participation from a range of local people and organisations (specifically those engaged with environmental and rural issues and practices, art and culture including Gaelic culture). The programme of broadcasts was transmitted from *Outlandia*, 4–9 August 2014, 12–4pm. The project blog site was updated daily and listening posts were set up at LADA's Study Room in East London

Fig. 8 *Outlandia* with satellite dish, 2014
Source: Inga Tillere

and at Caithness Horizons in Thurso and there was a link to the live broadcasts from the Edinburgh Art Festival website. The entire programme series lasting 20 hours and 7 minutes was repeat broadcast on 25 August 2014 and 26 December 2014. *Remote Performances* sought to transmit experience of place to diverse audiences from remote and wild locations through a series of live broadcasts, blog posts and a publication, encompassing art, music, performance and dialogue.

What follows in this publication is a record of the *Remote Performances* project, the commissioned artists, writers, poets, musicians and their art making strategies, performative and reflective responses to *Outlandia* and the surrounding landscape. The eclectic and diverse range of contributions includes poetry, fictions, images, sound works and dialogues that variously explore relationships between culture, technology and the human and animal world; poetry and fictions relating to landscapes of history and memory and parallel worlds; soundscapes engineered by the elements; physical expressions of engagement in place.

Fig. 9 Peter Lanceley with tooway satellite, 2014
Source: Inga Tillere

REFERENCES

Fraser, Malcolm (2011) 'Outlandia Fieldstation, Glen Nevis', *Architects' Journal*. Republished on *Outlandia* blog. Available online: http://www.outlandia.com [Accessed 7 Jan 2015].

Gilchrist, Bruce and Joelson, Jo, eds. (2005) *London Fieldworks: Little Earth*. London: London Fieldworks.

Outlandia blog. Available online: http://www.outlandia.com [Accessed 7 Jan 2015].

Remote Performances blog. Available online: http://www.remoteperformances.co.uk [Accessed 5 Jan 2015].

A Survey of the Terrain

Francis McKee

Fig. 10　*View of Ben Nevis*, 2014
Source: London Fieldworks

You head north up into the beyond, aiming towards Fort William. There is a choice of bus or train and either journey is spectacular. If you're like me though you will be lulled to sleep by the rhythm of the engine, waking sporadically to glimpses of forests, lochs, sheer hill rocks, waterfalls, eagles and docile lines of sheep. It's almost hallucinogenic: you cross many borders, a few of them are geographical, but most of them stray into other levels of reality.

When you reach Fort William shock sets in. The bus and train terminal is beside an endless sprawling Morrisons supermarket. It has everything you might need to camp in the wilderness, to climb a mountain or to drink yourself to oblivion. Deprived of their buses most people line the walls outside the shop, eating their sandwiches and supping cans of coke or lager. Through a concrete underpass lies the town's main street, scarred by poor planning and banal architecture.

Fort William is known in Gaelic as *An Gearasdan*: 'the garrison' in English. Originally established by Oliver Cromwell, after the English Civil War, it was one of three highland forts designed to suppress Jacobite uprisings. That garrison sensibility still lingers, roundhead functionality settled in the foothills of the country's most imaginative landscape. And that's the paradox that runs down the glens and up the mountain tracks in this region. At the very least there is always a binary phenomenon at play here: the twin mapping of the locale in English and in Gaelic; the soaring heights of Ben Nevis, Càrn Mòr Dearg, Aonach Beag and Aonach Mòr and the 'visitor experience'; the quest for wifi and a good pub in the shadow of peaks variously translated as 'venomous' and 'the mountain of heaven' (known to be the seat of the queen of winter).

Even in the history of the people who come to climb the peaks there is a sense of two worlds colliding. The famous Creagh Dubh Mountaineering Club founded in 1930 was composed of workers from the Glasgow and Clydebank shipyards who escaped from the industrialised city to the wildness of the highlands. Perhaps they can be seen as early emigrants from the grid, a process that has accelerated as the industrial skyline has been demolished and replaced with a less visible but more ubiquitous network of electronic and social forces.

The Creagh Dubh Club was one of several that transformed Scottish mountaineering and produced iconic figures such as John Cunningham whose career eventually took him to Nepal and the Antarctica where he became the first person to climb Mount Jackson. Ben Nevis, though, and the surrounding massif remained, and remain even now, central to the Club's excursions. Cunningham himself was swept to sea from the cliffs at Holyhead but Nevis claims many deaths each year. The mountain has a track that allows a constant stream of visitors to make a relatively easy ascent in the summer months but this lulls some walkers into lethal complacency, attempting the ascent in sneakers and equipped only with a mobile phone. Glen Nevis can be equally as dangerous at times but the mortality rates only seem to add an extra edge to the region, confirming its status as 'wilderness'.

However this liminal area might be described, it does provide access to insights and imaginative states of mind that cannot be reached so easily in cities. The planting of the *Outlandia* treehouse in the forests of Glen Nevis delineates a solitary space, suspended in the air like an architectural antenna. One of the projects carried out there for *Remote Performances* – Mark Vernon's collaboration with London Fieldworks: *The Sound of Lochaber* – challenges the notion of the silence of that wilderness. It seems quiet until the human ear recalibrates to subtler registers – animals, rain and wind, the sounds of a farm, the leaves rustling in the trees. Our senses adapt, opening up in the broad sweep of the landscape, and honing in more deftly to the nuances of its acoustics.

Another London Fieldworks' project – *Little Earth* by Bruce Gilchrist and Jo Joelson – draws part of its inspiration from the development of a cloud chamber by the Scottish scientist C.T.R. Wilson. In 1894, working in an observatory on the top of Ben Nevis, Wilson witnessed the spectacular optical effects produced by the Brocken Spectre – a phenomenon where the sun projects the shadow of the viewer onto clouds, haloed by rainbows. His attempts to explore the phenomenon in the laboratory led eventually to the development of a glass cloud chamber in which he could track sub-atomic particles (Gilchrist and Joelson, 2005).

It's ironic that the epic panoramic landscape of Lochaber focuses the mind on the almost imperceptible physical events that underpin the sense-altering physics of the place. It's also subversive: that impact on our senses encourages a recalibration of values concerning the environment and our place in it. The Creagh Dubh Club already demonstrated the lure of Ben Nevis and the surrounding area to workers immersed in the industrialised zones of Scotland. Later generations linked that hunger for natural landscape to the counter-cultural ideologies that emerged across the West in the 1960s and the 1990s.

The suggestion that this might be subversive is made more evident by recent moves against 'off grid' communities in the United States. In 2013 SWAT teams were brought in to close 'The Garden of Eden Community', a self-sustainable off grid collective in Texas. In early 2014 living off the grid was made illegal in Florida City where it was mandated that all homes must be connected to municipal water and electricity utility companies. Beyond the attempt to enforce links to corporate interests, these moves reveal a deeper anxiety concerning a citizen's right to shape their own lifestyle rather than conform to a particular social model. As many off the grid situations could be seen as innovative and experimental it also highlights the entropic planning sensibilities of governments and cities.

Perhaps this is one of the most compelling reasons to introduce artists to an off-grid project such as *Outlandia*. Given that experiment, innovation and adaptation are basic to a contemporary artist's practice, it's an ideal landscape to work in. That is not to say that artists will approach it simply as a utopian possibility. The contemporary world is too complex to envision Glen Nevis and its surrounding mountains as a romantic or escapist landscape. In his commentary on M. John Harrison's novel *Climbers* (2013), the well-known travel writer Robert Macfarlane analyses the author's approach to contemporary British landscape:

> This is a late-Thatcherite England – mostly northern – of contamination, industry, unemployment and discard. To evoke it, Harrison creates a language in which the natural and the artificial are fully fungible. Dribbles of ice on winter rock are 'shiny as solidified superglue'. Hedge mustard is 'stark as a tangle of barbed-wire'.

> *Everywhere, the toxic and the beautiful twine or swap with one another: in a public lavatory in spring, the 'cubicles [are] full of the smell of hawthorn, strange and lulling in a place like that, which overpowered even the reek of piss'.*
>
> *This is landscape writing, but not as we know it: descriptions so scoured of the delusions of the pastoral and the grandiosities of the sublime that the places they record seem surreal for being true. Harrison does this repeatedly, stripping back conventions to leave places skewed and startling. (2013)*

Harrison is best known as a science fiction and fantasy author but, as Macfarlane also points out in his introduction, *Climbers* shares his approach to all landscape as alien and dislocated. In a later novel, *Light* (2002), Harrison describes a series of worlds in which many types of physics operate independently of each other with no sense of overall harmony. This approach could stand as a model for artists approaching the many-layered world of Lochaber.

It is, in the end, a dialectical zone where many wild things bloom and multiply. Oliver Cromwell recognised this fertile and subversive potential as early as the 1650s and consolidated his Fort William in opposition to this fecundity. The tensions remain today and burst open at the slightest opportunity. *Outlandia* stands as an alternative outpost, even its name suggesting a place beyond the norm and beyond the borders of the status quo. It is a place that increasingly more of us need to visit and a place that offers a refreshing argument to the traditional white cube gallery where, as Robert Smithson put it, 'Works of art seen in such spaces seem to be going through a kind of esthetic convalescence' (1972). While Smithson wrote that as long ago as 1972, the criticism remains relevant as part of a long history of artists challenging the use of gallery space. Fresh air has always played a strong role in Scottish therapy but linked to the contemporary undercurrents of change swirling around politics, culture, science and the environment a journey to *Outlandia* now offers a welcome dose of alien dialectics.

REFERENCES

Gilchrist, Bruce and Joelson, Jo (2005) *London Fieldworks: Little Earth*. London: London Fieldworks.

Harrison, M. John (2013) *Climbers*. London: Gollancz. First published 1989.

Harrison, M. John (2002) *Light*. London: Gollancz.

Macfarlane, Robert (2013) 'Rereading Climbers by M. John Harrison', *The Guardian*, 10 May. Available online: http://www.theguardian.com/books/2013/may/10/robert-macfarlane-rereading-climbers [Accessed 28 Dec 2014].

Smithson, Robert (1972) 'Cultural Confinement', *Artforum*, October. Reprinted in Flam, Jack, ed. (1996) *Robert Smithson: The Collected Writings*, Berkeley/London: University of California Press. Available online: http://www.robertsmithson.com/essays/cultural.htm [Accessed 27 Dec 2014].

Kelpies, Banshees and Pibrochs Heard in these Parts

Geoff Sample

Fig. 11 Geoff Sample, *Remote Performances* broadcast, 4 August 2014
Source: Inga Tillere

Although the predominant theme in my sound recording work lies in the voices of other creatures, I'm particularly interested in the wider scene, the contextualisation: the arrangement and movements of these voices and other, elemental sounds convey a spatialisation of the landscape, a kind of sonic geography. Set within this modality is the emotional connection it creates in a human listener for whom there is so much cultural history connected with wild sounds, especially from birds here in the cooler latitudes, and the way they bring a landscape to life. However, you need calm, clear and quiet conditions to hear into the distance and grasp such articulation of living space on a large scale.

The weeks of later July 2014 were pretty benign for much of the British Isles. The sun was shining and it was warm. A proper summer. The weather forecasts for the West Highlands reckoned this would last up to the weekend of the 2nd/3rd of August, then growing changeable for the week of the performances, with some stormy swirls coming in. So I headed north on the Friday for my field work, ahead of my official sessions, and what I hoped would be a fine, calm dawn next day to listen and record in Glen Nevis. To discover the acoustic particularities of this iconic glen.

I've had a passionate interest in Highland ecology and wildlife since childhood, probably stemming from my first bird-book as a kid, and its landscapes-with-birds pictures, through fishing Scottish rivers with my grandfather, to many recording sessions over the last 20 years. So this felt a rare opportunity to be invited to take part in *Remote Performances* and produce some radio pieces immersed in the complex of sound and psychology that fixes these landscapes in the mind.

And, though a fairly quiet time of year in terms of the wildlife, it was a great dawn. Absolutely calm and surprisingly cool, giving rise to some smokey wisps of mist, but as the sun took over, it warmed to a perfect midge environment. There was a strong sense of vast aqueous space; but there was also a scattering of biophonic elements, as the tiny wrens mapped their spaces, distant young buzzards squealed for food and small groups of various songbirds, chaffinches, bullfinches, redpolls and crossbills moved through the woods. But what intrigued me most, as the morning rolled on, was an exotically-coloured line reaching diagonally up the lower slopes of the Ben: hundreds of people setting out on the path to climb the big mountain, like a kaleidoscopic millipede or some pilgrimage to the gates of heaven.

THE GLEN

> A short detour into Glen Nevis will provide a preview of the monolithic scenery hereabouts – scenery which has been compared in stature with that of the Himalayas by W.H. Murray, the well-known mountaineer. He sees in the Nevis Gorge a peculiar combination of cliff, woodland and water unparalleled in Britain and reminiscent of the Nepalese valleys. 'Ben Nevis, which at this point creates the highest amplitude of relief in Britain: an almost continuous slope of 4,000 feet descends from its summit to the valley floor'. (Whittow, 1977, p. 218)

I wanted to begin my pilgrimage in Glen Nevis, the location of *Outlandia* and the focal point of *Remote Performances*, and from there explore what the Highlands represent for me and how sound influences that construct. So I immersed myself in the idea of a 'glen' and its class of soundscape, so Scottish, though somewhat riven with the romance of Brigadoon.

I browsed various authors talking about the Highland soundscape and two themes emerged – silence and the elements, wind and water.

> *It was a permanent, living silence. Thunder, driving rain, and keening wind were sounds which seemed to emanate from it and fade back into it … the sudden bark of a deer or cry of a whaup only served to emphasise its depth. It was a vast, unseen but ever present reality. (Farre, 1957, p. 10)*

> *The sound of all this moving water is as integral to the mountain, as pollen to the flower. One hears it without listening, as one breathes without thinking. But to a listening ear, the sound disintegrates into many different notes – the slow slap of a loch, the high clear trill of a rivulet, the roar of spate. On one short stretch of burn, the ear may distinguish a dozen different notes at once. (Shepherd, 2011, p. 26)*

But I was also aware of how a glen was living space, a frame for life. The glen was a community's home, self-contained, remote and often separated from neighbouring communities by high ground. Also the space of the glen acts acoustically as a frame for any songs or calls of creatures that occur within it; and somehow impresses those sonic events more deeply on the senses, the sparseness of its biophony imbuing a particular intimacy with the listener.

> *A pair of black-throated divers were resting on the water a hundred yards away, unafraid of me. Then they rose to go back to their nesting loch, and the acoustic quality of the place enabled me to hear the sound of their movements, amplified but clean-cut … When a hind barks here, the deer of two hills are alert … (Darling, 1937, np.)*

SEASONS, ECOLOGIES AND COMMUNITIES: HIGHLAND AIRS

Yet, considering my own fieldwork experiences, I felt that while this elemental 'silence' may be a general underlying condition, the soundscape of a glen is very much dependent on ecological factors (how close to the coast, the underlying geology, the amount of woodland) and the season. The Highlands have provided me with many memorable creature concerts through being at a certain place at a certain time.

It might be a gathering of various waders en route to their breeding grounds on the estuary at the head of a sea-loch in spring, their excitement audible as they settle in to roost at dusk, or the midnight chorus of corncrakes spread out through a Hebridean meadow in mid-summer, or a large flock of finches gathered under beech trees in a feeding frenzy as dusk approaches, bringing the long fast of a cold winter night. Community gatherings.

> *Upstairs was one big room, which contained four beds, three of them made by the master of the house, and all seven children slept there, huddling like a litter of*

> *pups and listening, in their respective season, to the gales, the corncrakes and the roaring of the stags. (Cameron, 1988, p. 21)*

I finished this piece with *Homo sapiens* at play – a fishing party's dusk chorus on a summer night when I was recording black-throated divers. They'd obviously dined well at the hotel on the shores of the loch, then rowed out in the gloaming to the ruins on a small island – as it happens, the last stronghold of the Wolf of Badenoch, a notorious outlaw of the area in the fifteenth century. And there they charged the landscape with their voices, sounding for the echo.

MYTHOLOGISING

> *Some feel there's a sadness in the glens.*
> *The emptiness. The piles of stones.*
> *A home for moss and lichens,*
> *Where there was a house in the once-upon-a-time.*
> *You think you catch the laughter of children in the distance -*
> *But it's only the voice of the river.*

For my third piece I wanted to move into the ways the Highland landscape has influenced the cultural mythologies of Scottish identity. The Acts of Union early in the eighteenth century and then the subjugation of Scotland with the battle of Culloden opened the way for the first tourist accounts of the Highlands from Thomas Pennant in 1769 (2000) and Johnson and Boswell in 1785 (1984). Coming so soon after James Macpherson's controversial publication of his Ossianic cycle of poetry, the Highlands became fertile ground for the imaginations of the Romantic painters and their patrons. This flow of mystique gained strength again in the early twentieth century with the proliferation of the motorcar, and found expression in the wealth of guide books published since the 1930s.

And at the time of *Remote Performances* we were perched on the cusp of a big question for the Scottish people. Yes or No. A question of identity: Scottish or British? The referendum on independence was six weeks away and Pat, who was helping out at the house we were staying in, was actively involved in bringing together the disparate Scottish Left into a unified stance pro-independence. Her knowledge and eloquence on Scottish culture and history informed the general discussion round the dinner table.

The changing weather conditions during the week created some spectacular lighting effects between the mountain slopes and the clouds, the rains enhancing the velvety lushness of the summer vegetation. And there were some periods of absolute calm which spread the lochs with other-worldly reflections. The scenery was genuinely awesome in these conditions, creating an appropriate mood for contemplating the influence of the landscape on the whole tradition of writers and artists swept up in the sense of the sublime, so palpable in these parts.

All that Scottish gestalt was flowing through my mind on the evening when Tony White gave us a performance of his 'Stormbringer' story, to the backdrop of a large window through which we gazed out to the Hebridean island of Rum, once 'the forbidden island', personal playground of a Lancashire industrialist. Tony gave a passionate incantation conjuring up the febrile imagination of a rock star holed up on another Scottish island. I loved it.

Somehow for this third piece I slipped into the ancient medium of augury – seeking guidance from observing birds. A practice that swept through the prehistoric cultures of Eurasia, possibly evolving from shamanic traditions, but culminating in the debased political office of augur in classical Rome. Yet the ideas still linger. From Cole Porter's *Every time we say goodbye*: 'why do birds up above me, who must be in the know …'. And with it the idea that birds move between two worlds, this and the other, and can tell us something of the hidden agenda – messengers of the gods.

> *And birds just know. They come and go.*
> *They move through that subliminal space,*
> *somewhere between earth and heaven.*

I called on cuckoo, raven and stag, three iconic figures in Celtic and Scottish mythologies (and beyond) to give guidance on an undefined question. The ancient seer Teiresias, Deidre of the Sorrows, James Macpherson, Edwin Landseer, Seton Gordon, Frank Fraser Darling, Hamish Brown – all came to mind, in the quest for connection between soul and land, through their interpretation of natural phenomena. And the pilgrimage to climb The Ben became a metaphor for questions of personal and national identity.

> *It's autumn. And there's a roaring in the glen.*
> *It may be the wind. Or the river in spate.*
> *Or the voice of the deer.*
> *It's that time of year, that time of life.*
> *You've just got to let it out.*
> *It's Game of Thrones: Who will be Monarch of the Glen?*

Did it all work? There were a few technical problems here and there; and maybe my material was looser than I would have liked. But the spirit was there. And, sat up in *Outlandia*, going out live, something clicked. It felt good. Connected. The remote here, through me, reaching out tendrils to other remote places. But connected too with such a diversely inspired gathering of artists.

Maybe we go remote, into the wilderness, to escape the human network, yet paradoxically get closer to ourselves and our animal being.

NOTES

My title is from Thomson (1938) *Bens and Glens*.

REFERENCES

Cameron, Archie (1988) *Bare Feet and Tackety Boots: A Childhood on Rhum*. Barr: Luath.

Darling, Frank Fraser (1937) *A Herd of Red Deer: A Study in Animal Behavior*. London: Oxford University Press.

Farre, Rowena (1957) *Seal Morning*. London: Hutchinson.

Johnson, Samuel and Boswell, James (1984) *A Journey to the Western Islands of Scotland AND The Journal of a Tour to the Hebrides*. Harmondsworth: Penguin. First published 1785.

Pennant, Thomas (2000) *A Tour in Scotland*. Edinburgh: Birlinn. First published 1769.

Shepherd, Nan (2011) *The Living Mountain: A Celebration of the Cairngorm Mountains of Scotland*. Edinburgh: Canongate Books. First published 1977.

Thomson, Stewart (1938) *Bens and Glens: Wayfarings in Scotland*. London: Clarke.

Whittow, J. B. (1977) *Geology and Scenery Scotland*. Harmondsworth: Penguin.

Like Like

Michael Pedersen

Fig. 12 Loch Eil, 2014
Source: Courtesy of the artist, Michael Pedersen, and Ziggy Campbell.

Like the little fences cast around crumbling rock
and the barricades sprung up to hold back
the landslides of the future, I, too, am standing tall,
bearing weights and burdens; like the fast flash
camera of the coach-full aimed inexorably at every
peak and billowing cloud; and the caramel
hair, systematically brushed, of the young girl on
the 08:21 from Glasgow to Fort William who alights
at Roybridge; and the freshness of the royal
blue in the old carriage made new which now stands
monument and idle – a flower bed at best; like
the wooden geese that pepper nearby gardens
and each painted pig boasting myriad grins gained, and
admiration over aptitude for stars; like the bruising
in the sky before a triumphant burst of rain
that frankly should be honoured by trumpets and
French horns galore; like the fierce gradients, inclines
and ascensions on my molars, pre-molars and half-in
wisdoms – precipices conquered by mine own pink tongue
and just one or two others; like their electric roots
which will only cause more pain as time goes on
and will never be ancient and will foster and promote
an imperfect bite, which I wouldn't bother criticise –
there's just no time; like every kilo of collapsing scree
and the thousand things in eyeshot that've been
mossed over til the seasons change; like red
rowan berries through gangling gorse and
razor blade fences tearing tiny pockets in
the hovering air; like months from now when frost
is needling and parliamentary gusts howl out
and there's sloshing and shrieking in the silver
circuits of wind somewhere just above head-height;
like the old Aussie tourist ambling nearby on a
once in a lifetime trip his antipodean wife had always
wanted to take; the trip to craggy, scratchy, full-blossomed,
blistering Highlands Scotchland – she's maybe
watching now, giddy, a goofy grin, cheering him on
and drinking in every detail in unison,
but then again, mostly likely she's not;
like the accidental cappuccino
ordered in Lochaber Café whilst debating who to phone
and declare a safe arrival to and to declare
an I miss you to and to be able to say I'll be back soon

and to warn them not to over water the plant in the
living-room which survives and remains verdant
and lush despite long absences and little losses;
like a lugubrious lake while the loch's lilted
in a simple three letter shift; like an ox-bow
pining for the passing river or Scafell Pike becoming
an ever bigger bump post a ballot box binge;
like all bonds being best left to tectonics; like the way
Ziggy's late and whisky-soaked but smoulders
something together in no time at all; a
lit cigarette emptying itself, burning bare;
like a veritable crossroad, no really, left or right
which fucking way are we heading; there's humour
in all their soggy wee sheep faces, but sadness too;
with no idea blood congeals into delicious
pudding; like southern rupture on northern planes;
like how I could swear I saw the chimney pipe
of a rogue submarine pop up and out
the water on the way back to the lodge
but at 40 miles per hour
who can be sure; especially when trees melt
into long filigree veils and once they distance and
clear, once they've lifted their skirts and we steer
towards a different patch of water with less movement
that's more brightly beamed upon, who can be
sure of anything so transitory; like walking upwards
into moist alpine in suede shoes unfit
for pretty much anything steeper or wetter than
city summer; and I'm breathing through my teeth
so as not to swallow any flies, tongue
pawing at the crevices of my incisors, pushing
at the cracks like a daft dog unaware of its fleshy
abundance, daggering into the mellow inlets
until a small trickle of blood seeps out and reminds
my mouth and body how every motor runs
down eventually; then we're drinking at dinner
and I'm prompted to mention how I let you down
by drinking too
much, dropping your hand at key moments,
again, then again;
like the semblance of a synergy, in a listless
way, when perhaps, truly, there was no such
closeness to speak of.

Selections from *The Hut Book*

Alec Finlay

Fig. 13   *Circle Poem (for* Outlandia), 2010
Source: Courtesy of the artist, Alec Finlay

Fig. 14 *Sweeney's Bothy*, Isle of Eigg (Alec Finlay and The Bothy Project), 2014
Source: Lucy Conway

(I)
WHAT IS A HUT?

a hut is
four thin walls
nailed around
a hot metal stove

•

a hut is
set in the fret
of green woods

•

a cabin is
spied
on the wild-hills-
   ide

SELECTIONS FROM *THE HUT BOOK*   27

•

a hut is
framed wilderness

•

a hut is
make-do-and-mend –

it grows in an
organic fashion
as a collage of accretion
*   and borrowing*

•

a hut is
a second home
which there is
no shame
*   to own*

•

a hut is
a sounding-
board for rain
which will do you
no harm

if you remember to
spoon out
the guttering

•

a hut is
an excuse
for tea

•

a hut is
a tree-high dissension

.

in Scotland
where we are so proud
of our welcome
huts have regrettably
not been

(II)
HUTOPIA

Han Shan's Hut

I cut some thatch
to roof my hut
dug a pool and runnel
for the spate

now I'm old and bald
alone on a dim ridge

free to go anywhere
with my sore legs

settled in my hut
I sigh for the tide,
today, yesterday,
all the years
gone by
aye

Hjertoya

Schwitters's
wee window
sets an angle
as do the hills

Shuibhne's Oratory

A full house couldn't
be more lovely
than my little oratory
in Tuam Inbir
hid within hazel,
fern and bramble

Where the stars are
set in order together
with the sun and moon

A house where the rain
does not pour in
a place where spears
are no longer dreaded

My wee hut's
as bright as a garden
but there's no wall
to fence me in

Prospect Cottage

Jarman's neat cabin
on the shingle jut
of Dungeness

Derek is gone
his garden
grows on

Sweeney's Bothy, Bothan Shuibhne

the thorn
is the riddle
that we began
our design from

a memory
of Shuibhne's spear
and the harsh brang
of battle

how will we bring
the thorn
into translation

so that it can flower
into dwelling?

how will we enter
Sweeney's aviform vision
exchanging beak and wing
for turf and beam?

The Bothy (Inshriach)

the wee stove gets so hot
the shower's been put
on the outside

Carbeth

'Things come to rest here'.
  – Gerry Loose

just a wee felt-roofed hut,
a shame to stay inside
but there is rain

wisps of white smoke
rise straightforwardly
from the chimley,

those yaffles
they must be trying
to laugh their way in

there's lovage and angelica
too strong tasting
for deer or rabbits

last year's tansy
buttons that fashion
this spring's brown

Dumgoyach seems
only a few steps away
but I'll just sit on
this handy log
drinking smoky tea
and wait a while
for the windfalls

Outlandia

a stand of spruce
cleared to make
a hut of larch

this hut has a mast
this is a crow's nest

this shoogle-shack
will give you vertigo

this hut scrapes
carousel clouds

a frottage cottage
an angel's wing

for all those
who take the path,
what lies before you
is silence,
what comes after you
is silence

Fig. 15   *Inshriach Bothy*, Cairngorms, The Bothy Project, 2013
Source: Luke Allan

NOTES

Han Shan's Hut: These lines are composed after Gary Synder and Burton Watson's translations of the Chinese mountain hermit, Han Shan's *Cold Mountain*.

Hjertoya (1934–1939): Kurt Schwitters's hut and installation in Norway.

Shuibhne's Oratory (twelfth century): After 'The Pity of Nature', from a version of the *Shuibhne Cycle* by an Irish Monk of the twelfth century, published in *A Golden Treasury of Irish Poetry;* the oratory is Shuibhne's tree, in which he sleeps.

Prospect Cottage (1987–1994): Derek Jarman's wooden cottage where he created an innovative garden featuring coastal flora.

Sweeney's Bothy, Bothan Shuibhne (2013): The second of The Bothy Project bothies, in collaboration with Alec Finlay. Located in Cleadale, Isle of Eigg, the bothy offers short artist residencies. Sweeney, the mad warrior king and poet, inspired the design, which incorporates a raised bed on a thorn-like platform.

The Bothy, Inshriach (2011): The first of The Bothy Project bothies, near the Cairngorms.

Carbeth (2013): Gerry Loose and Morven Gregor's hut in the self-styled People's Republic of Carbeth. This poem was composed for *The Road North,* in collaboration with Ken Cockburn (2014).

Outlandia (2010): Conceived by London Fieldworks, designed by Malcolm Fraser Architects, built by Norman Clark, 2010. Ken Cockburn and I chose *Outlandia* as one of our locations for *The Road North*, pairing it with the Japanese mountain temple of Ryushakuji. It is one of the key representatives of the hutopian movement, an avant-garde version of hutting.

Angel's Wing: *Pleurocybella porrigens,* mushrooms, picked on the walk to *Outlandia*.

REFERENCES

Finlay, Alec and Cockburn, Ken (2014) *The Road North*. Bristol: Shearsman.

From a Train

Goodiepal

Fig. 16 Goodiepal, *Remote Performances* broadcast, 9 August 2014
Source: Inga Tillere

TRANSCRIPTION OF A SOUND FILE RECORDED IN A NIGHT TRAIN FROM FORT WILLIAM AND SENT FROM LONDON UPON ARRIVAL THE NEXT MORNING

'Here's Goodiepal speaking and I will try to say something clever here from the train. I have been cycling a lot and I have been distributing sound files which are part of a book I published two years ago. The book is full of riddles that work together with sound files and it is called *El Camino Del Hardcore – Rejsen Til Nordens Indre* (2012). It is a book that has been distributed among very adventurous people in the electronic and computer music world. In order to distribute my files I came up with a theory which I still believe is true and I think it is the only intelligent thing I have ever said. I think it is almost an equation and it goes like this:

> *The further a message has to travel over space and time the more importance you can add to its content.*

I think this is really true.

Imagine if you received a piece of recorded information back from ancient Egypt – there is no way that cannot top anything done by the Beatles for example, but then again anything done by the Beatles will always top anything done by me – simply because it has travelled further over space and time. Since I have been doing things for quite a while everything I do will have a certain power simply by having existed and when a person listens to it, it has travelled through a certain period of time. If you add space to that then it becomes much more interesting. Let's say you receive a message from the stars. Such a message will by far be the most important message ever received by human beings simply because it has travelled so far.

What happened in *Remote Performances* was very interesting. Resonance 104.4fm were transmitting over space but not time. Of course time was involved but it was superfast satellite communication, next level action. It did not deal with the concept of delay and I think they could have benefitted from that. For instance what would have happened if they just recorded all the broadcasts and brought them to London on a hard drive and played them on a radio station down there? Wouldn't that have been the same? Would that even have been more interesting because you could have said this happened two or three or five weeks ago. Or what would have happened if all the recordings were placed in a container and left for 20 years and then broadcast. Would that have made them more interesting? That is something to think about and that is what I tried to play with by saying ok let's send a sound file the fast way and send a letter with information as well the slower way and let both things match up at the end and see what comes out of that (see Plates xxx–xxxi).

I think time is of great importance in communications these days but very few artists playing with broadcasting and transmitting deal much with the concept of time. Very few people working with digital media also deal with the concept of gettting old. There's something about time that is almost phased out in modern day communciation. Does that make any sense?

FROM A TRAIN 35

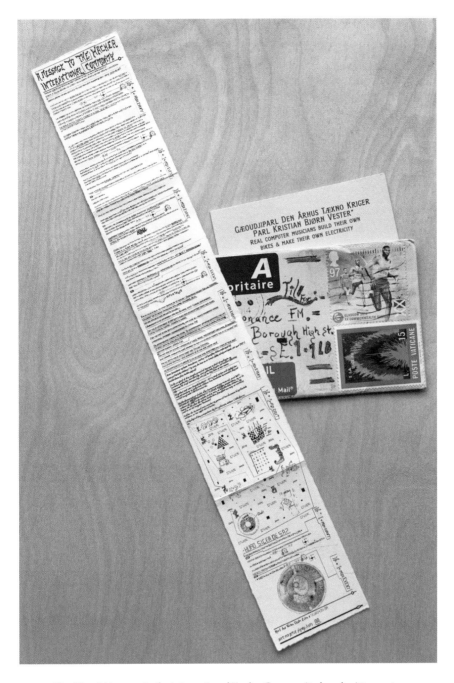

Fig. 17 *A Message to the International Hacker Community*, handwritten note, 2014. Half of the artwork was performed live in radio broadcast at *Outlandia* and the other half was sent by post to Resonance 104.4fm in London and placed online as an image-file, to enable the decoding of the message
Source: Courtesy of the artist Goodiepal and London Fieldworks

Thinking about remoteness: sometimes instead of going and playing concerts myself, I have instead sent a package that can be unfolded at the venue over time and then I will, for example, phone up and give instructions to unfold certain objects or certain feature sequences over time and thereby create an atmosphere which is alive at the moment when it happens. In that situation people are gathered at the listening place and the event takes place at the listening place rather than at a remote area. I don't know if it is better but it is different. If I do a show in Berlin and feel I pollute the environment too much by going in person, then I might do a show by sending a few things and asking them to unfold them, then that is a fixed concert venue with me being the imaginary other, undefinable performer somewhere. In the wilderness you are very remote but remote from what? Is remoteness an urban dream?'

REFERENCES

Goodiepal (2012) *El Camino Del Hardcore – Rejsen Til Nordens Indre*. Copenhagen: Alku.

The Sound of Lochaber

London Fieldworks and Mark Vernon

Fig. 18 Arisaig Highland Games, August 2014
Source: London Fieldworks

Silent walk	Wilhelmina war 1746 Campbell	Different accents
Car pass and arrive at hall	Cow poo on the line delay	Charlie wind and rain
Train to Lochailort	Train wait for piper to finish	Leicester dipper birds in silence
Walking away	Gate half open half expect train	Somerset bagpipes feel in heart
Norway	Loch Mordor meaning water	West Midlands water sheep
Bucks chocolate	Loch Sheil level gauge readings	Dutch wind through woods and sheep
Paris teens	Charlie laugh	Sheep
West Midlands box tick	Foot of Ben Nevis gate	Dutch sound of silence
France go to top	Path walk	Water on rocks
Holland underestimate	French busker chat and tune	Close up and foamy
German well prepared	Laughter Ingrid	What is Ingrid English
Bottle bank	Laughter	Ingrid Gaelic
Busker walk-by subway	Museum commandos film music	Gaelic whisper
Canoe surface drag	Smoking duck breasts	What is Paisley
Paddle	Steam	What is smokehouse lady
Dogs not let people on train	Steam train	What shop
Route and bit throat out	Whistle only	Accordion end
Place of bodies	Duck lady sheep sounds	Angels' share
Kinlocheil and Tarbet and Glenfinnan	Nature sounds	Auction bell
Sun glint on loch	Ingrid Gaelic and traditional music	Banging workman
Geology survey readings	Owls and ships and peace	Bee smoker
Gauge found	Paris different accents	Beeps
Skilled drovers	Polish girls silence	Tune
Commandos run Germans	Scot the brave Gaelic	Bell auction
Norway bomb bridge mistake	Bagpipes proud to be Scot	Bells cow

Postman had to deliver coat	French busk bagpipes	Bucket and stool
Name high rocky place	Birds in tree	Restoration
Butter barrel	Girdle and feather brush	Closest
Churn	Milking fake cow	Off into distance
Churn glass	Jetson hello echo	Bagpipe end
Cheep	Accordian bass	Chug hiss
Chirp of joy	Music slow	Cup rattle
Churn glass	Backward slow ghostly	Gun
Cockerel crows	Gathering intro	Bagpipes
Barrel roll and load onto tractor	Music group	Pigeon shoot
Cask vehicle reverse beeps	Breakdown only	Walk round race announce and fair games
Open door	Song	Strongman bells
Ingredients and process	Milk cow first time	Race boys and girls
Mash	Mountain stream	Bagpipe triangle
Fermentation echo chamber	Paolo Berardelli	Last call under nine girls and race
Wood vats filled with water so don't dry out	Piano broken	Missing piper
Mind body tail cows half cut	Pour water into cow	Race results walk round and seniors race
Barrel technique	Milk cow	Dance with piper
Distillery bells	Singing sands	Atmosphere with MP
Double bass	Sheep bleats on farm	Ceilidh Trailers
Drag step ladder	Smelt pipe	Warming up
Fill cow slow	No rain	Plughole train loo with and without water
Hens and chicks feeding time	Water pipe	Rattly bits
What was that used for	Standpipe outflow	Scrappy bits
Butter churn glass	Swallows feeding chicks	Rattly and scrappy bits
Cow bells	Idle whistle and start up again	Lighting a fire

Black pudding vein cutter	Front very noisy fast tunnel passes	Fire
Surge	The gathering very distant	Steam blast
Fade in and out	Closer	Embers
Whistle only	Interior atmosphere with chatter loud clackety and two whistles	Washing machine
Steam train fast	Rattly teacups	Hiss
Hiss and doors	Nice clackety interior to gentle halt	Room thirteen kids
Engine idling hiss	Metal bin rattle and walk through compartment to train stop	Gondola
Idling whistle toot and shunt	Short loud surge	Coming round the mountain song
From pause to speed	Fast to slow pull into end	Malcolm Fraser
Getting faster	Passengers disembark engine steam then moves off	Singing sands
Rhythm	Train bass from steam	Snow goose Ben Nevis highest mountain
Passing walls at speed flutter	Tone	Waves on rocks
Fast and whistle stop and man exit train	Train chug	Ben Nevis streams
Idle to start chug with whistle	Clackety squeak	Water through glen
Clickety clack and whistle and faster and faster	Train fast chug	Birds tweet fireworks mum kitchen brother yawn
Interior clacking near engine	Weird bangs under train with seagull	Hissy fit
Steamy hissing at slow speed	Clacks getting faster inside to out window chug	Can someone turn tap
Getting up to speed	Carriage atmosphere chatter train stop	Burn
Creaky in-between and whoosh short	Whistle groan hiss	White noise
Creaky in-between longer	Boardwalk gravel walk	Underwater
Short clacks to fade heavy	Boat and bird	Louder

NOTES

The Sound of Lochaber was a six-part radio broadcast made for *Remote Performances* by London Fieldworks and Mark Vernon. The programmes, which were broadcast over six days, were titled The Gathering, The Angel's Share, Highland Games, Songlines, The Jacobite and Distillation. The preceding list of sound descriptions was generated from the file names of audio field recordings made at the following locations: Achindaul, Great Glen Cattle Ranch, Spean Bridge; Gleann Leac na Muidhe; Sound of Arisaig; Jacobite steam train (Mallaig–Fort William); The Rural Education Centre, Torlundy; Arisaig Highland Games; Glen Uig Smoke House; Loch Ailort; Nevis Range; Loch Linnie; the Ben Nevis Distillery, Fort William; the Loch Eilde Mor hydroelectric generating station, Kinlochleven; Glenfinnan; Fort William High Street; Roshven, Lochailort (see Plates xxii–xxiii).

Some of the recordings featured the voices of (amongst others): Paolo Berardelli; Lila Berardelli; Isabel Campbell; Malcolm Fraser; Ingrid Henderson; Jetson Joelson Gilchrist; Charlie MacFarlane; Joe O'Connell.

Geo Graphy

Tracey Warr

Fig. 19   Arriving at Lochailort Station, August 2014
Source: London Fieldworks

1. PERVERSE RADIO

For the *Remote Performances* project in August 2014 I travelled to *Outlandia* in Glen Nevis from Toulouse taking a train and then a plane and then a bus and then another train that I stepped from at midnight onto a tiny, rain-lashed, unmanned station in the Highlands. Was I remote yet? Was I in nature? Jo Joelson picked me up and we drove forty minutes further north. Deer crossed the dark road ahead of us in a long, leaping stream. A young stag stood guard in front of them turning to face us in the headlights, staring us down until the herd had cleared behind him. I was in his territory now.[1]

Remote Performances consisted of six days of live radio broadcasts from Glen Nevis by 20 invited artists who work with sound, visual art or text, along with broadcasts by people from the local community in Fort William and Lochaber. The six days of broadcasts created a portrait of this specific place, but a portrait with echoes and resonances for many places elsewhere. For that week the Glen resonated with its bird and animal calls, paralleled by the calls of artists via the Resonance104.4fm live radio link. It was perverse to house a temporary radio station in *Outlandia*, a tiny off-grid space up a precipitously steep track with no road

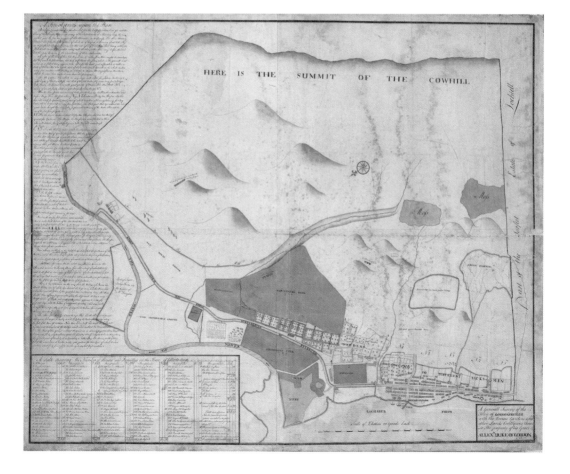

Fig. 20 Peter May, A *Generall Survey of the Town of Gordon'sburgh with the houses gardens and other lands contiguous there-to. The property of his Grace Allexr, Duke of Gordon*, 1753
Source: Reproduced by permission of the National Library of Scotland

access, necessitating the lugging of gear and the use of a gas-powered generator and satellite link so that connection to our invisible audience elsewhere always seemed precarious. Miraculously *Remote Performances* only fell off-air for a few short bursts during the six days, occasionally affected by the vagaries of weather conditions. The technology had to work with and adapt to its surroundings.

Several layers of translation occurred in *Remote Performances*, from place to radio broadcasts by artists, and then from sound broadcasts to images and texts in this book. This essay tracks the place through these filters of translation and artists' performances, to find what place we wound up in at the end of the journey.

2. SOUNDING THE PLACE

The place – the Highlands – has a loaded history of grievous contestations. In his broadcast, historian Alex Du Toit from the Lochaber Archive Centre in Fort William talked about the Clearings and the Jacobite Risings.

> *From early on Lochaber was recorded by the authorities in London as the most savage and difficult area to deal with. They used to call it The Rough Bounds. It was occupied by many of the most important Clans involved in the Jacobite Risings including the Macdonalds and Camerons. They often fought each other too. It was regarded as a chaotic area. Knoydart is the last wilderness in Britain, inaccessible by road, you can only reach it by boat from Mallaig. During the Civil War in the 1600s Fort William was built by Cromwell's men. After the revolution in 1688 a new fort was built to keep an eye on the Clans in the area. A whole chain of forts was built up the Great Glen including Fort Augustus and Fort George. It was an area with a great deal of violence and opposition to government in its history. (Du Toit, 2014)*

Today Lochaber Archive Centre often receives visitors from the Scottish Diaspora – people from Canada, Australia and New Zealand looking for information on their ancestors. The contemporary Highlands are overlaid with their real and fictive histories: a local carpark is named after *Braveheart* which was filmed here, and Harry Potter chased the quidditch up the Glen and over the viaduct on a broom stick. Other contemporary visitors walk the West Highland Way, enjoy the 'UK's Outdoor Capital', the Iron Man competitions, join the 150,000 people who climb Ben Nevis every year, tour the Distilleries. Yet despite these mediations, packagings and enscribings it seems hubris for anyone to presume ownership of this place. The inhabitants are only slightly less temporary, less frivolous, than the tourists in the scale of things. As Land Artist Robert Smithson put it: 'Fragments of a timeless geology laugh without mirth at the time-filled hopes of ecology' (Smithson, 1972, p. 152).

The *Local Spot* broadcasts expressed a depth of intimate knowledge and proximity with this place: a forester's carefully observed account of antnests in the woods; sheep farmer Ian McColl with his finely carved horn shepherd's crook, its handle worn glossy and marbled from the slide of a hand over the years; the anecdotes of veteran mountain rescue volunteers; Ingrid Henderson playing the clàrsach; a young cèilidh band and other local musicians (see Plates xii–xix). *The Sound of Lochaber* by London Fieldworks and Mark Vernon was another portrait of the place. In a daily series of magical broadcasts we listened to the sounds of milking cows, shearing sheep, reducing duck fat, a cockerel's crow, the animal auction bell, a whiskey distillery, the Jacobite steam train. Meanwhile the waters and winds of the Glen continued their own unremitting theme tune.

Within The Highlands, the other place we were performing in was *Outlandia*, a small and simple off-grid wooden space suspended in the forest, facing the looming mountain, 'The Ben' as it is affectionately known to locals, on the opposite side of the Glen. *Outlandia* is itself an artwork created by London Fieldworks. It is an evocative, immersive space provoking creative responses from other artists, writers and practitioners in a range of disciplines. Over 30 artists and writers have undertaken residencies at *Outlandia* since it opened in 2010 it has also been used by geographers, foresters and school groups.[2] It is a secluded space immersing its occupants in a forest and mountain landscape. You approach it up a very steep track and along a boardwalk above a peat bog, surrounded by trees, mushrooms, midge and birds. The steep climb means you have to come carrying little with you, except your senses and your thoughts.

Outlandia creates an intimacy with its surroundings and the seasons, as you watch weather coming fast up the Glen, crossing the face of the Ben. It is often in the clouds. *Outlandia* is a nest, a bothy, a tardis, a place to experience landscape as animate. The appeal of sheds and huts is their inside/outside paradox. It is also a place of withdrawal and generation – a creative space in the tradition of structures such as Goethe's Gartenhaus in Weimar, Henry Thoreau's cabin at Walden Pond, Dylan Thomas' writing shack in Laugharne and other examples of generative, ephemeral architecture that Alec Finlay refers to in 'Selections from The Hut Book' on pp. 25–31. Numerous artists' residencies in remote places attest to the effectiveness of remoteness for focus and reflection, to generate ideas. These remote creative cradles and nests in turn refer to ancient hermit monks and desert fathers who sought solitude to contemplate and praise Creation (see Colm Cille and Macfarlane, 2008, pp. 23–32).

Importantly *Outlandia* is as much an imaginary, fictive place as it is a real one. It continues suspended in the mind's eye as a visual longing when you are absent from it. Place is always part reality, part imaginary. *Outlandia*, Goodiepal remarked, is an urban dream: a romantic, magical treehouse, architect-designed, hanging in the trees with a view of mountains, visually expressing a hankering for a return to childhood, escape from social convention and rules, immersion in Another Green Place. It is a microcosmic expression of a world and a life we would like to make and have that is so very different from the world we have made and move within.

3. REMOTE NATURE

What is remoteness, where is it, why might you need it, and how can you get there if you do need it? Arriving at the artists' base house in Roshven on the coast with a stupendous view of the sea and the islands, I was confronted by a kitchen full of artists, laptops, booms, cameras and tripods. Is anywhere truly remote?

If remoteness means geographically distant, we have to ask distant from what? Is Fort William in the Scottish Highlands distant from London or is London distant from Fort William? How distant does remoteness need to be? A geographical definition of remoteness is relative to the locatedness of the person doing the defining, or it assumes the notion of centre and periphery. A city dweller might find most rural areas remote, but a person from a rural area may need something more extreme to register as remote for them. Walkers, cyclists, river swimmers, boaters, and mountain climbers, will have a different sense of what is inaccessible than an habituated motorist. Is remoteness a place where there is no human trace 'except the rim of my own eyes' (Macfarlane, 2008, p. 60)? In remote nature, such as The Highlands, you can feel and see Earth's rhythms more clearly than in the city.

The human species has regarded itself as the master of nature. Nature was imagined as something outside of us, something we mined, dammed and harnessed; that we riddled with roads, railways and flight paths. And then we realised that we are part of nature after all and as Earth started to suffer from an overload of human toxic production, we realised that we will be living with the legacies of our own activities: rising global temperatures and sea levels, threatened water and food supplies, air and water quality.[3] We have created and are living in the Anthropocene – a new geological era where human activity has transformed geology, the chemistry of the sea, soil and air, and the climate (see Working Group on the Anthropocene; Steffen et al, 2011; Schwägerl, 2015; Latour, 2014; Linke et al).

In 1900 the human population was 1.7 billion and by 2010 it was 6.9 billion (Steffen et al, 2011). E.O. Wilson claims 'The pattern of human population growth in the twentieth century was more bacterial than primate' (2002). Macfarlane writes, 'In Britain, over sixty-one million people now live in 93,000 square miles of land. Remoteness has been almost abolished'. There are, he says, 30 million cars and over 210,000 miles of road (2008, pp. 9–11).

Does a place have to be technologically disconnected, off-grid, to be remote? Connectivity and disconnection depend on material and economic factors as well as geographic and topographic ones, on the infrastructure of phone lines, pylons, mobile signal masts, satellites and various sources of power. Being 'cut off' has changed its meaning. An artist is as likely to seek technological disconnection as geographical remoteness: to disconnect from the daily demands which mostly come down a wifi connection. Our technologies are prosthetic by now, a natural part of the human animal.

Macfarlane argues that there is a human need to connect to wildness. Why is it useful for artists to be at least temporarily solitary and disengaged? For focus, to disable procrastination and because creative generation loves a vacuum. Unplugged from daily routines and networks, the self becomes a strange new locale for exploration, reinvention, and reportage.

Might remoteness be a psychological state as well as a geographical or technological one? City remoteness might be in the suburbs, in the view from high above, in the middle of the night, on the river, in a prison, in the canopy of trees in a park, or in some process of defamiliarisation, of well-worn ruts made strange.

Being a walker is an estranged position. 'In the world, but apart from it', writes Rebecca Solnit, 'with the detachment of the traveller rather than the ties of the worker, the dweller, the member of a group' (2001, p. 21). *Outlandia*, similarly, is a place that is in the world but apart from it. And it is a place that operates 60 per cent as a real location and 40 per cent as a conjured imaginary. Much Land Art operates on this basis too, as places of vivid familiarity from photographs and descriptions but little footfall.

Remoteness is temporal as well as spatial. We talk of the distant past and the remote future, and of a different sense of time in remote places: slower, more considered, more humane perhaps, away from the urban pulse. In both rural and city environments seasons can impact on a sense of remoteness: with winter bringing more 'remoteness', more risk of disconnection.

The history of remoteness encompasses Enlightenment voyages of discovery and colonialism, which Clair Chinnery engages with in her work, eliding the territories of invasive, parasitic cuckoos with the territorial behaviour of humans. The Romantics escaped from rapid changes in the city and country wrought by industrialisation. Carolyn Merchant argues that our foundational mythologies concern either a return to, or a progress to, the Garden of Eden (1980). The notions of dystopia and utopia also revolve around these myths.

Contemporary Remoteness[4] incorporates a sea-change in our attitudes towards Nature which has moved from something to be kept at bay, something fearful, something to be exploited and manipulated and controlled, to something we long for. And just at the moment of our longing we realise there is no such thing as Nature out there. We have been 'putting something called Nature on a pedestal and admiring it from afar' (Morton, 2007, p. 5). Timothy Morton describes our attitude as a 'sadistic admiration' of Nature. We imagined that we dominated nature, as we conquered territories and new frontiers. Now there is a crisis in humans' relationships with their surroundings. 'We would be unable to cope with modernity unless we had a few pockets of place in which to store our hope' (Morton, 2007, p. 11). Morton unpacks the complexity of our creation of 'Nature' and our relationship with that construct. 'One of the basic problems with nature is that it could be considered either as a substance, as a squishy thing in itself, or as an essence, as an abstract principle that transcends the material realm and even the realm of representation' (2007, p. 16). Nature it seems, needs to be protected from us, and at the same time, it is itself red in tooth and claw as Alfred Tennyson put it in the nineteenth century as he engaged with Darwin's theories of evolution and the survival of the fittest: 'nature has been used to … inspire kindness and compassion, and to justify competition and cruelty' (Morton, 2007, p. 19).

Examining remote nature in their work in Glen Nevis, artists Lee Patterson, Benedict Drew and Lisa O'Brien foraged up the Glen for sound, and Geoff Sample stalked the sound of the Glen with a practised ear. Drew responded to the layers of mediation overlaid on the Glen, creating a critical take on what is Nature now and our relationship to it. Sample comes to his understanding of nature through the nature writing of Frank Fraser Darling, Archie Cameron and Rowena Farre, and through maps. Several pieces created for *Remote Performances* evoked our projections of horror and fear onto nature – Johny Brown's story of succubi with a twist, and Ed Baxter's murderous vision. Tony White's story, 'High-Lands', on the other hand, conjured nature as a place of refuge and refusal. In Italo Calvino's novel *Baron in the Trees*, the Baron takes to a life in the trees, never touching the ground, but declares that his choice is not a withdrawal from society but rather a resistance to social conventions and inequalities (1959).

Human relationships to Earth shifted significantly in 1784 with the invention of the steam engine and the inauguration of the industrial revolution, and then again in 1945 with the invention and explosions of atom and nuclear bombs. And since then large-scale impacts on 'Nature' have included the Chernobyl nuclear accident, the Deepwater Horizon oil spill in 2010, and everything suggested by the discovery of the Great Pacific Garbage Patch. There is no outside or elsewhere to nature, no here and there. We simply are in it, in continuity with everything in it. Morton coins the term 'hyperobjects' to describe 'things that are massively distributed in time and space relative to humans' (Morton, 2013, p. 1) such as the biosphere, the Solar System, the human species, global warming, styrofoam and plastic bags, capitalism, oil, radiation – they are not forever, he says, but they have very large finitude. Patterson's soundwork emphasised this entanglement of the human with the natural. Made on the shores of Loch Ailort and in Glen Nevis, Patterson's work mixed 'natural' sounds with human and especially technological noises: the drama of thunder and rain alongside the sounds of a failed satellite connection and the conversation of the anxious, coping radio crew: 'don't worry' … 'what's that Sarah?' … 'What have we got now?' … 'Nothing'. Cutting in amidst waterfall, water drips, the pulses of underwater life, were thrummed piano strings, a tapped microphone.

Several of the artists created work emphasising nature as animate. Patterson recorded, amplified, composed, conducted sounds in nature that we cannot usually hear. Sarah Kenchington's pneumatic euphonium enabled us to hear the sea breathing in melodic wheezings, groanings, snorings and huffings. The sea's spit swirled inside Kenchington's wind instrument. Bram Thomas Arnold tried various means of creating dialogue with Nature – swearing an oath to it, reading physics, philosophy and poetry to it, and frustratedly throwing rocks at it when the other side of the dialogue was hard to hear.

4. MAKING PERFORMANCES

Morton writes: 'it is in art that the fantasies we have about nature take shape – and dissolve' (2007, p. 1). He argues that 'in no sense … should art be PR for climate change' (2013, p. 196) so what then can and should art be in relation to climate change and the Anthropocene? Art can be a way to critically encounter what we cannot see or touch, the hyperobjects of global warming and the biosphere. The twenty artists working with sound, visual art and text, who made work for *Remote Performances*, addressed the current state of Nature through creative research rather than scientific study.

The twenty artists were creating 'performances' – some kind of creative response to the surroundings – very quickly and under pressure. They arrived, they engaged in a brief research process with the place, and made something in response in a rollercoaster of making, editing and broadcasting. The artists came from The Highlands, other parts of Scotland, the Faroe Islands and Denmark, and from England and Wales. Between these artists and the local collaborators and contributors a complex portrait of the place emerged in the broadcasts: reflecting back to Lochaber inhabitants their own experiences and contexts, and expressing outsider longings for a far and different place. *Remote Performances* captured hereness in Glen Nevis from many angles.

Outlandia is a little hut in the forest, but it became a big performance space for that week – cramming in several bands, a harp, a host of live guests, and broadcasting to an international audience. One dictionary definition of performance is 'A display of exaggerated behaviour or process involving a great deal of unnecessary time, effort and fuss'. Brown and Baxter's radio dramas; Barker's electric performance, retelling ancient myths of the land (see Plate xxxiv); Alec Finlay and Ken Cockburn's performed panegyric to the landscape, *The Road North* (see Plate xxxv); Michael Pedersen's outdoor poetry slam; and White's performance of *Stormbringer*, where words rolled and rollicked like pebbles in the surf; these were all exaggerated and necessary performances.

In the 1990s Hal Foster described the artist as ethnographer (1996), but now the artist is more geographer as the disciplines of human geography, human ecology and eco-art elide. Geography and Art expand towards each other, from eighteenth century landscape painting to twentieth century art in the expanded field: Land Art, Site-specific art and Eco Art (see Hawkins, 2014; Kastner, 1998; Spaid, 2002). In the twenty-first century art engages with place through artists' residencies (see Further Resources on pp. 157–8), and through embodied practices such as walking art and other modes of artists working 'in the field'. Being in the field affects the processes that artists use to make work employing geographical tools and methods, including maps, map-making, fieldwork, and documentary practices. Art seeks to know, to feel a locale on the pulses through a practice of critically inhabiting place.

Art has become exploring, mapping and attempting to understand the space we are immersed in and impacting on. Maps do a lot more than help to get us from here to there. 'As travelers … we need to distrust the urge to scoop up theme and meaning, as if the things we can neatly pack are necessarily the things we came for' (Turchi, 2009, p. 97).

As part of the *Remote Performances* project I ran a Writers' Workshop focussing on mapping and walking with local writers.[5] In the Lochaber Archive we looked at historical maps of Fort William. The writers each brought along their own maps of places that held strong memories of experiences, or suggested imagined and future journeys. One writer brought along a map of the human anatomy. Some of the writers said they marked up maps using them as a sort of diary or log. We looked at the text on maps and map legends and used them to construct pieces of descriptive writing and stories. We imagined our way into the maps. Map Reading OS Explorer 392 Ben Nevis and Fort William: forest, stone, hill, ford, cairn, ridge, waterfall, stepping stones, gully, shelter.

Later we walked in the Glen, making and taking four sentences for a walk. 'What if the sentences were characters?' asked Nuno Sacramento and he wrote:

Four sentences walk into a bar.

Nature my arse. The cars flying past on the road next to the telephone poles. There is the rumble of an airplane. While we walk, we edit this out to look for the 'nature'.

Walking up a path. Never leaving the path.

Deep listening with eyes closed. An engine. Human voices getting near. Feet dragging over the gravel. Sounds become words. More feet. Bird song. Voices disappearing into sounds.

Back at the car park. Tree stumps. Large trees. Managed trees? Where there were trees there are now spaces.

Art is not illustrative, it is critical and often research-led. Its research processes are promiscuous, so Chinnery reads sixteenth-century books, looks at bird corpses in a museum, imagines being a bird, builds a human-size nest, sings with birds in the forest; Arnold stands in rivers and woods, sits on hilltops, grappling with philosophy and physics; Baxter watches sheep-dogs at work; Kenchington clambers over wild rock-strewn beaches, collaborating with the sea; Kirsteen Davidson Kelly collaborates with a local music teacher and a shipwright; Brown keeps his ears open in the pub; White transposes other times, other places onto his Highland surroundings; and Barker identifies with geology and ecology.

The artists in *Remote Performances* explored the terrain bringing back diverse reports: Patterson's sound compositions of organisms from mollusks to the human animal; Sample's sonic geographies; Pedersen's foray into the landscape of the Highlands and the landscape of his own emotions; O'Brien's daily expeditions into woods and weather; Goodiepal's enquiries into our urban dreams and our sense of time.

Contemporary Remoteness has a new role to play in helping artists, curators and writers contemplate, represent and mitigate the issues of the twenty-first century. Art 'in expanding the world of our imagination beyond the world of our experience, allows us a more intimate – and so more thorough, and perhaps more compassionate – imaginative knowledge … than we are likely ever to have in the course of our daily lives' (Turchi, 2009, p. 157). A place is made from its histories, its present communities – human and non-human, its topography, its connections, its future. The artists in *Remote Performances* listen, look, sense and tell us stories about the human immersion and entanglement with place. Since cave paintings, bards, skalds and troubadours, we have told ourselves stories of human entwinement with place.[6] Radio satisfies the old need to hear these stories. Radio whispers its voices and sounds intimately into your ear, seeming to speak only to you.

REFERENCES

Calvino, Italo (1959) *The Baron in the Trees.* New York: William Collins.

Colm Cille's Spiral. Available online: http://www.colmcillespiral.net [Accessed 6 Jan 2015].

Du Toit, Alex (2014) 'Local Spot Broadcast', *Remote Performances*, Wednesday 6 August 2014. Available online: http://www.remoteperformances.co.uk [Accessed 6 Jan 2015].

Foster, Hal (1996) 'The Artist as Ethnographer', in *The Return of the Real.* Cambridge, Mass.: MIT Press.

Hawkins, Harriet (2014) *For Creative Geographies: Geography, Visual Arts and the Making of Worlds.* London: Routledge.

Hoban, Russell (1980) *Riddley Walker.* London: Jonathan Cape.

Intergovernmental Panel on Climate Change (2014) *Fifth Assessment Report (AR5).* Available online: http://www.ipcc.ch [Accessed 6 Jan 2015].

Kastner, Jeffrey, ed. (1998) *Land and Environmental Art.* London: Phaidon.

Latour, Bruno (2014) 'Agency at the time of the Anthropocene', *New Literary History*, Vol. 45, pp. 1–18.

Linke, Armin; Territorial Agency & Franke, Anselm, *The Anthropocene Observatory.* Available online: http://www.anthropoceneobservatory.net/ [Accessed 15 Dec 2014].

Macfarlane, Robert (2008) *The Wild Places.* London: Granta.

Merchant, Carolyn (1980) *The Death of Nature.* New York: Harper Collins.

Morton, Timothy (2013) *Hyperobjects: Philosophy and Ecology After the End of the World (Posthumanities).* Minneapolis: University of Minnesota Press.

Morton, Timothy (2007) *Ecology Without Nature: Rethinking Environmental Aesthetics.* Cambridge, Mass.: Harvard University Press.

Schwägerl, Christian (2015) *The Anthropocene.* London: Synergetic Press.

Solnit, Rebecca (2001) *Wanderlust: A History of Walking.* London: Verso.

Smithson, Robert (1972) 'The Spiral Jetty' in Smithson, Robert (1996) *The Collected Writings.* Berkeley: University of California Press, pp. 143–53.

Spaid, Sue, ed. (2002) *Ecovention.* Corte Madera: Greenmuseum.org.

Steffen, Will; Grinevald, Jacques; Crutzen, Paul and McNeill, John (2011) 'The Anthropocene: Conceptual and Historical Perspectives', *Philosophical Transactions of The Royal Society*, 369, pp. 842–67.

Turchi, Peter (2009) *Maps of the Imagination: The Writer as Cartographer.* San Antonio, Texas: Trinity University Press.

Warr, Tracey (2014) *A Study Room Guide to Remoteness*. London: Live Art Development Agency. http://www.thisisliveart.co.uk/blog/a-study-room-guide-to-remoteness/

Wilson, E.O. (2002) 'The bottleneck', *Scientific American,* February, pp. 82–91.

Working Group on the Anthropocene. Available online: http://quaternary.stratigraphy.org/workinggroups/anthropocene/ [Accessed 6 Jan 2015].

NOTES

1   Parts of this essay have evolved out of my Blogposts written during *Remote Performances* in August 2014 http://www.thisisliveart.co.uk/blog/remote-performances-day-1-what-is-remoteness and the writing of *A Study Room Guide to Remoteness* for the Live Art Development Agency (Warr, 2014).

2   Artists' residencies at *Outlandia* since 2010 are documented on http://www.outlandia.com

3   The 2014 *Fifth Report of the Intergovermental Panel on Climate Change* notes 'unequivocal and unprecedented warming of Earth's climate system': atmosphere and ocean have warmed, amounts of snow and ice have diminished, sea levels have risen, concentrations of greenhouse gases have increased. 'Most aspects of climate change will persist for many centuries even if emissions of CO_2 are stopped. This represents a substantial multi-century climate change commitment created by past, present and future emissions of CO_2' (2014).

4   The nascent term 'Contemporary Remote' has been developing through a series of recent projects by artists London Fieldworks focussing on the proliferation of objects and technological colonisation which they see as central to an idea of the contemporary remote. http://www.remoteperformances.co.uk/post/90462180644/post-digital-contemporary-remote

5   The writers participating in the workshop were Nuno Sacramento, Alison Lloyd, Gillian Ness, Anne Claydon-Wallace, Gay Anderson, Carol Brock and Lorna Finlayson.

6   See Russell Hoban's future fiction, *Riddley Walker* (1980) where storytelling is a central theme.

There's a Monster in the Nest-box

Clair Chinnery

Fig. 21   *Boatswain's Call*, video still, 2013
Source: Courtesy of the artist, Clair Chinnery

From the start, *Outlandia* struck me as a human sized bird-box, perched high in a remote forest canopy. Hence, my proposal for *Remote Performances* to build a nest in this 'hut'- a curious structure, the interior of which is physically and visually inaccessible for those without a key. There is a window, offering spectacular views of Ben Nevis, which are only afforded to its privileged inhabitants (whoever they might be), but you can't 'look in' because of an un-scalable drop to the ground below – so steep is the hillside on which the hut stands. When opened, however, the window resembles the large aperture of a box made for monster-sized Robins, and other birds that dislike the restrictions of nest-boxes with knot-shaped holes. The interior space – incredibly tall, in comparison to the square footage of the floor space and topped by a skylight – allows freedom of movement, access and action that goes beyond human scale and habitation. Standing, sentinel-like, on the engineered pillar of a coniferous trunk – a giant version of suburban bird boxes, perched atop tall garden posts (safe from the reach of murderous domestic cats) – *Outlandia* prompts imaginary questions. What monstrous bird might live here? And what terrible predators might the hut keep out?

A nest. A simple idea it would seem, except that for me, this opportunity had the potential to yield far more than the material act of making a human-sized nest. In realising *The Human Nest-box* (versions of which were created on-site in both 2013 and 2014), I was able creatively to extend an existing body of work based on a longstanding fascination with birds. Even in urban environments, their voices permeate our sound world like no other animals, reminding us that they are never far away. They have a general disrespect for human attempts to 'put them in their place', transcending – by virtue of evolutionary adaptation – the laws of physics as well as geographic and national borders. They have often appeared in my work, and have recently occupied a major focus through key projects. *Cuculus Prospectus* (2011 onwards – comprising sculptures, prints, drawings, video and site based actions) examines the parasitic behaviours of the Eurasian Cuckoo, *Cuculus canorus*. Here, I explore these evolutionary adaptations as metaphors of historic and continued legacies of European colonialism, migration and shifting ecologies. Central to my project is an exploration of 'hybridity', with a recent focus further exploring the commonality of human and non-human impulses. These impulses, both used and referred to in *Cuculus Prospectus*, are also central to the work made for *Remote Performances*.

As an extension to *Cuculus Prospectus,* my work at *Outlandia* has a direct relationship with two of my previous works, *How to Speak …: The Breeding Birds of the United Kingdom* (2000) and *Briefe and True: Lost Landscapes* (2005). *How to Speak …:* is an Artist's Book and Audio-work, where I hybridised selected information found in ornithological field guides, and language learning materials, subsequently filtering these sources through text-to-speech software. In *How to Speak …:* issues of migration, and the acquisition of language were investigated in addition to explorations of taxonomy, especially with regard to ideas about national identity and inclusion/exclusion.

Briefe and True: Lost Landscapes was completed in 2005 following visits to Fort Raleigh National Park in NC, USA. Between 1584 and 1590 English voyages were made to Virginia (now coastal North Carolina) in an attempt to further the Elizabethan expansion and colonisation of the New World. In 1585 Thomas Harriot and the artist John White made a scientific study of the plants, animals, inhabitants and minerals of the area. In 1590 Harriot published their findings in his illustrated *Briefe and True Report of the New Found Land of Virginia*. Partially designed as a 'prospectus' for English colonists and including descriptions of exploitable New World resources, it pictured a remote place for the domestic imaginary. The supposed site of Walter Raleigh's 'Lost Colony' is central to the history and narratives of colonial North America. My *Briefe and True* specifically responds to Theodor de Bry's published 'modified versions' of John White's watercolour studies of native Algonquian peoples, which appear in Harriot's 1590 *Report* (Harriot, 1972). Remoteness was further conventionalized by de Bry for a European 'homeland'.

Cuculus Prospectus re-imagines Thomas Harriot's *Report* from the perspective of a Eurasian Cuckoo. I researched colonial and parasitic behaviour in plants and animals, and especially birds in order to extend such Early Modern ideas, additionally investigating more recent discoveries and practices in natural history, taxonomy, animal and/or human migration, colonial impulses and global environmental change. I was also interested to develop ideas expressed in Alfred Crosby's book *Ecological Imperialism* (1986) which explores and illuminates how the ecosystems and topographies of various parts of the modern world have been shaped by human colonial interventions (intended or otherwise).

Cuculus canorus has one of the most sophisticated and adapted parasitic behaviours in the avian world. 'Brood parasitism' is a phenomenon made famous by Cuckoos, which annually migrate to Britain and Europe from Africa in order to breed. Naturalist and ornithologist Ian Wyllie has documented the bird's parasitic process (1981). Female Cuckoos remove one egg from a host's clutch with their beak, then immediately lay their egg in the nest before departing – hopefully unnoticed. Cuckoo eggs are usually the first in a clutch to hatch and the primary urge (or reflex) of the blind and naked Cuckoo chick is to eject anything else (usually another egg or hatchling) so that it can be raised as a singleton chick.

An astonishing and sophisticated adaptation of *Cuculus canorus* is its ability to use 'egg mimicry' to 'fool' hosts into accepting its egg as their own. *Cuculus canorus*, can mimic the eggs of a great many host species, with a wide diversity of egg coloration and size. Cuckoos are genetically identical (that is, all the same species) and are notoriously promiscuous breeders. Yet females will usually parasitize only one of many host species, and this will differ from one female to another.

Cuculus canorus is found in Europe, Asia and Africa but nowhere in the Americas. Discovering this prompted me to reconnect further to Harriot's *Briefe and True Report* as a *'prospectus'* selling a New World of imaginative and commodifiable possibilities to would-be English colonists. 'Remoteness' became saleable. I imagined a scenario in which an 'Old World' migratory bird would go about planning the extension of its breeding territory into another 'new' continent. In developing this idea, I was explicitly thinking about the extent to which human colonisation has affected plant and animal life on earth – species whose habitats and ranges have, and continue to, extend, shift and diminish. I therefore attempted to occupy the 'hybrid' mindset of both 'Human' and 'Cuckoo'. This produced a strange, conjoined logic through which various individual works could imaginatively take shape. I wanted my research processes and archival experiences to 'inhabit' the artworks that would make up *Cuculus Prospectus* though it was impossible to determine how this would happen.

The major archival research for this project took place at Oxford University's Museums, Alexander Library and the ornithological archives of London's Natural History Museum [NHM] (based at Tring, Hertfordshire). The latter has one of the world's oldest and most comprehensive collections including specimens collected during Scott's Antarctic expedition, and the pigeons bred by Charles Darwin. The archive is a product of European colonialism and the accompanying 'human behavioural' drive for taxonomy and order at home and abroad – remoteness codified. During my research, I became interested in the compulsive nature of the scientific and empirical archiving methods used to store, separate and organise the many thousands of skins, skeletons, nests, eggs and spirit specimens in the national collection. In one of the stacks I was shown a 'collection' of host nests parasitized by *Cuculus canorus*. At Tring, eggs are separated from their nests as part of the NHM's archival protocol. Again, visually and physically this 'action' has an effect, above and beyond a seemingly prosaic archival method.

As a research process, *Cuculus Prospectus* consequently became immersed in the authoritative empiricism of the scientific archive, and its historical conventions and forms. The juxtaposition of these with the conceptual and imaginative grounding of my practice, produced, for me, an 'approach' or 'behaviour' or 'mindset'. This resulted in the development of what I refer to as 'pseudo-scientific' criteria through which my imagined avian New World colonisation could be filtered, and a *new* list of *potential* Cuckoo hosts could be made using a combination of empirical data and documentation on *Cuculus canorus* and 'Human' colonial motivations and reasoning.

Through the archival research undertaken, I was able, in all, to find evidence of 107 species of European hosts to *Cuculus canorus* (including anomalies). Selection criteria for potential 'New World' hosts were thus identified, taking account of:

1. Breeding season
2. Egg gestation period
3. Nest accessibility
4. Egg size
5. Diet
6. 'Altricial' host young
7. Latitudinal breeding range
8. Temperament
9. Avoidance of communal or colonial breeders
10. Disregarding rare/possibly extinct species.

Using these criteria, *all* the species of birds of the North American land mass were considered and narrowed down to 160 potential hosts for my imagined colonising Cuckoo. It is these species that are named in the various completed works that make up *Cuculus Prospectus*, which was first exhibited in 2011 at Beldam Gallery, Brunel University (then consisting of ten completed works). Two of these works have specifically served as resources which have helped to shape and determine the research process of the site based actions and interventions undertaken during my time in residence at *Outlandia*.

Firstly, and most importantly *Cuculus Prospectus: Host Nesting Materials Archive* (2011) is an equivalent to an empirically correct cataloguing system: 125 boxes, each contain a material used by the 160 potential North American 'Cuckoo hosts' for nest construction. The alphabetized archive separates materials used for outer nest, mid-layer and inner nest construction. Box labels and accompanying wall charts enable the viewer to cross-reference materials to species and vice versa, building a semi-imagined version of each host's nest from the perspective of the 'non-nesting' Human/Cuckoo. Secondly, *Existing New World Servants* (2011) overlays distribution diagrams (from field guides) of the North American territories of 14 European host species, common to both 'Old' and 'New World'. Although it looks like a recognisable land map, it contains no physical geographical information.

Empirically, both works served to inform and largely determine the work I made at *Outlandia* in both 2013 and 2014. I undertook various activities – relative to the 'remote' Highland site – in an attempt to further 'inhabit' the mind of my fictitious colonial Cuckoo. I used this opportunity to carry out what I have referred to as 'field operations'. Under the working title *The Human Nest-box,* a number of processes and actions took place in and around the hut, using the data set generated by *Cuculus Prospectus* to re-occupy the 'hybrid mindset' I had used in my earlier research process.

A major part of both visits to *Outlandia* involved improvised attempts to build a nest from a list of 30 known materials used by the 14 known and potential Cuckoo hosts common to both Old and New Worlds. This action provided an opportunity for me (as a creature with no experience of nest building) to immerse myself in a process alien to both Humans and Cuckoos. In this respect, the 'remote privacy' afforded by the hut enabled me to test out new and imagined inter-species survival strategies. I was reminded of manoeuvres undertaken by survival enthusiasts and the military in preparing for unforeseen future eventualities and environments. Both works (nests), entitled *Generic Highland Hybrid Host 1* and *2* were entirely made from materials found at or near to the site and were constructed in an improvised manner in response to both environment and the interior limitations/possibilities of the space. The height of the hut proved invaluable in enabling long sections of material to be brought into the space. Methods used for construction were very similar to those used by many species of bird, but took place on a much larger scale.

As the nests 'grew' the strength and engineering of their structure became apparent. When completed, the nests' 'bowl sections' were approximately 50cm above the floor of the tree-house and both nests were capable of holding multiple adult human occupants with ease. The 2014 nest eventually became much larger, assuming an 'inhabitable' space, closer to the interior architecture of the hut, and more accurately resembling the nest of a bird-box dweller. All materials used were carefully selected so as not to disturb the natural ecology of the forest. I used only

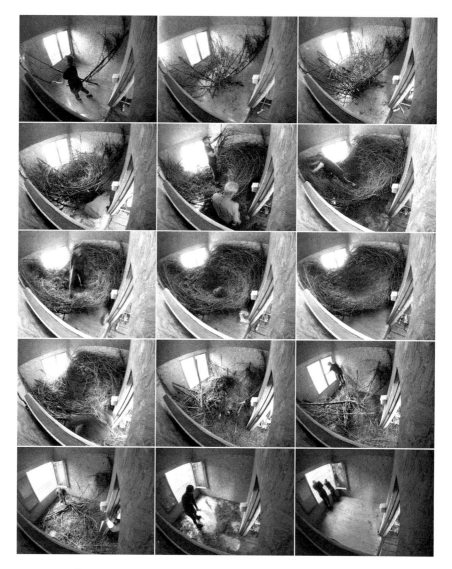

Fig. 22 *Generic Highland Hybrid Host 2*, timelapse sequence, 2014
Source: Courtesy of the artist, Clair Chinnery

fallen branches, twigs and other materials, and re-distributed these across the area at the end of the residencies. Samples of materials used were documented and catalogued according to the archival process used in previous parts of *Cuculus Prospectus*. These have been cross-referenced against known European and imagined potential North American Cuckoo hosts. This process revealed that the *Outlandia* nests share materials from many of these 'real and potential' hosts, but are in reality hybrid nests formed from the materials used by many bird species.

Whilst in situ, I used both 'nests' to develop performative actions, testing a set of 14 'mimicked' calls made by the 14 'common' Cuckoo hosts using the limited

Fig. 23 *Generic Highland Hybrid Host 2*, composite photo, 2014
Source: Courtesy of the artist, Clair Chinnery

capabilities of a 'boatswain's' whistle. These 'sound actions' explored the colonial aspirations of *Cuculus Prospectus* from a nautical and militaristic perspective via an untranslatable human methodology and device. For *Remote Performances* in 2014, I additionally re-performed *Boatswain's Call* at various loch-side and coastal locations (see Plates xxvi–xxviii). These new (but equally remote) contexts developed the specific instructional character of the boatswain's whistle as a 'call to arms' – in many cases eliciting vocal responses from resident birdlife! I further utilised the opportunity to extend my 'whistling actions' during *Remote Performances* by bringing together an accumulation of various whistles, collected over many years and manufactured for different purposes. These whistles collectively have four main (human) applications: discipline, distress, hunting and orchestral. In putting together whistles manufactured for different uses, documentation of these 'remote performances' bear witness to the genesis of an absurd, monstrous hybrid vocabulary.

Participating in *Remote Performances* enabled me to develop possibilities and opportunities to explore an ongoing fascination with 'hybridity' and 'mimicry' through various forms, including performance within 'remote' locations and environments – a 'New-World' metaphor. In modest and idiosyncratic ways, these works draw on the lessons of Crosby's *Ecological Imperialism* through contemporary art practice, using cross-disciplinary sources, strategies and conventions in unorthodox ways. Crosby's text reveals why the world has come to look, feel, smell and sound the way it does because of the adaptive capabilities of plants, animals and diseases, and the consequences of their global displacement. It reveals a world in which the accelerated pace of 'human' adaptation has led to colonialism, migrations (voluntary and forced), extinctions, assimilations and hybridisations. My 'remote performances' explore and 'inhabit' evolutionary, 'behavioural' adaptations as metaphors for the legacies of colonialism and resultant 'hybridity'.

REFERENCES

Crosby, Alfred W. (1986) *Ecological Imperialism: The Biological Expansion of Europe 900–1900*. Cambridge: Cambridge University Press.

Harriot, Thomas (1972) *A Briefe and True Report of the New Found Land of Virginia*, Theodore de Bry edition, with a new introduction by Paul Hulton. New York: Dover. First published 1590.

Wyllie, Ian (1981) *The Cuckoo*. London: Batsford.

In Search of Silence

Lisa O'Brien

Fig. 24   Lisa O'Brien, *Remote Performances* broadcast, August 2014
Source: Inga Tillere

I'm often asked 'How far is the nearest big supermarket?' Is that, I wonder, an accurate measure of remoteness? Can it be defined by proximity to supermarkets, evidence of human settlements or the ability to be in contact with other humans? Is walking for hours without seeing another person more remote than living in the middle of a city yet not speaking to anyone for days or feeling lonely in a crowd of people you don't know or lonely in a crowd of people you do know? Am I confusing remoteness with isolation? And where do isolation and remoteness cross over with loneliness? How does remoteness relate to wildness and wilderness?

I'm not always a fan of the relatively remote life I live in a village of 100 or so people. I'm an hour and a half from a large supermarket (in case you're interested) on the North West Coast of Scotland. It's a love/hate relationship, largely dependent on weather, opportunities, or lack thereof, hours of daylight and … the weather again. But, when the rain is horizontal and you fight 60mph winds to get the dog out for a walk, you certainly feel alive. On days when you see pine martens, white tailed eagles, stags and double rainbows from your window, you become acutely aware of the magic of the place. There are fictional lands I only read about in fairytales as a city child but sometimes, here, they exist. It is a wilderness and we are to some extent at the mercy of the land and the weather. Power outages, no running water and landslides are not uncommon due to rain and high winds and remind us of our human frailty.

In relation to an artistic practice, ten years of living in a remote and bleak landscape has resulted in a desire to strip things back to their bare essentials. Aurally and visually the aesthetic is often sparse. Psychologically it can be a harsh environment to negotiate. Iconic trees and strident electricity poles burn their outlines on to my retinas and function as markers to orientate myself. In vast swathes of the landscape the wind has blown away anything not tied down or firmly rooted. The fauna, stags and sheep have eaten much of the remaining flora. The former forests look apocalyptic after logging has befallen them. Where is the comfort, the protection and safe haven for the human in this landscape?

When considering remoteness, I imagine most people think of the wild places, where no other people or dwellings exist. I think that remoteness, in our imagination, is a quiet place yet, in reality, most remote and wild places are full of noise. Not human-made noise but wind, weather and nature, so why do people imagine that it is silent? Is it because that is what they want or need as an antithesis to city life or is it what they fear?

On the path to Steall waterfall in Glen Nevis, whilst searching with sound recordist Peter Lanceley for the silence symbolic of remoteness in my imagination, our ears seemed to search instinctively for sound (see Plate xxi). How do you listen to silence? It's like the negative space in a drawing and it requires a shift of perception to look at the space around the objects rather than the objects themselves. The silence comes in between the sounds but mostly it doesn't come at all, fleeting pockets of nothing. We gravitated towards running burns and rustling leaves and made futile attempts to record ephemeral evidence of quiet, and instead used noise to describe silence. This was an activity predictably doomed to fail. But we tried. And anyway, on that day amongst the tourists, this place did not feel at all remote.

Fig. 25 *Balgy Panorama left*, 297 x 210 mm, pencil on paper, 2014
Source: Courtesy of the artist, Lisa O'Brien

Remoteness is relative to your starting point. Where is the centre of remoteness, and is that a paradox in itself? How do we measure where the most remote place is, geographically, psychologically, metaphysically, metaphorically. And why does it have such allure and mystique?

Walking up through Glen Nevis forest to *Outlandia* the following day I was alone for the first time in 24 hours. For me it had been fantastic to get a chance to spend time with other artists and all too short. However, this was a project about remoteness and it was feeling anything but, due to crowds of visitors in the area. It was very different to how I usually spend my days, walking through local woods and forests for an hour or more each day and not seeing a soul and then working on my own from home. When I'm outside I draw, record and observe the changing weather and seasons, daylight hours. I film, think and have often dull, but occasionally inspiring, conversations going on in my head. It can be overwhelming, the landscape and the weather, especially when I stop to consider the thousands of years that the place I am stood in has existed largely unchanged. But the walking and the wilderness allow my brain some space to experience the sense of the place in motion, as a physical way of engaging with what's around me. Experiencing it 'now', rather than reflecting on the memory and the history of the place is sometimes more manageable.

In Glen Nevis, when I reached the boardwalk leading to *Outlandia* I entered a very grounded space where the trees thickened. There was barely any sunlight, but deep moss greens, the damp fusty smells of aged wood and the dense soft build-up underfoot of pine needles and humus. Sound was deadened, just dull crackling twigs, repetitive footsteps and my own heavy breathing from climbing the hill. Strong verticals created a protective barrier either side of the boardwalk outlining an area of tall almost cathedral-like space. Here there was a stillness and remoteness, despite knowing that before long I would arrive at the *Outlandia* treehouse, full of equipment and people. Without a map, just a few scribbled directions, I didn't know how long it would take to get there and for a few special metres, time was suspended. There was an awe about the place, a metaphorical silence and wonder at the feeling of remoteness, isolation, solitariness.

Sometimes the remote landscape functions so clearly as metaphor for the human condition. It might reflect or contribute to your state of mind. From the single lonesome wind-beaten tree, to the ravaged broken woodlands and then the dense inner sanctum or paradoxically hidden terror of the deep forest, the landscape is loaded with meaning, and how we connect to it psychologically and physically is a rich area for exploration.

In the past, when I lived in the city, I would have avoided solitary forays into woods and forests as I felt out of my comfort zone. Despite that, living and working in the Highlands means I am now often in woods on my own. I'd never properly considered why I had this unease, but going to *Outlandia* provided a focal point for me to mull it over.

Entering dense forests feels like stepping into the unknown, there can be a sense of foreboding due to unrecognisable sounds and trepidation at what or who may be behind the trees. The underlying sense of threat seems to be hardwired. Perhaps it's a primitive response, a survival instinct. Or it might be from childhood, growing up with myths and folktales such as Little Red Riding Hood, living and breathing Enid Blyton's Enchanted Forest series and Grimm's fairytales inspired by the Black Forest in Germany. In 'Sleeping Beauty' for example, based on a fourteenth century folktale, the prince has to conquer the 'evil' forest. This forest is the realization of the wicked stepmother's curse. Later I moved on to Hammer House of Horror (still recovering) and old classics on TV such as Count Dracula with Christopher Lee. The Carpathian forests of Transylvania (sylvan means woods or forest) loomed threateningly in my young imagination.

My actual experience of woods as a child was many happy hours spent in Firth Park in Sheffield with a small gang of friends, grass sledging, dam building in the streams, generally roaming about, going to the fair and kids school holiday club. But there was always an underlying threat when walking home alone as for a long time there were reports of a man committing sexual offences in the woods and we were definitely not to talk to strangers. The forest continues to be a major protaganist in horror films such as *The Blair Witch Project*, and more recently in Lars Von Triers's *Antichrist* (see Zolkos, 2011), neither of which I've been brave enough to watch all the way through. The forest is often a major part of the narrative in a story and is used to evoke intense anxiety and threat. In reality the forest can be a wild and untamed place, uncultivated by humans and potentially unsafe. The lack of recognisable order means we are facing the unknown. In large wild forests, it is easy to get lost physically and therefore perhaps there is also a fear of mentally unraveling.

Fig. 26 *Torridon Forest, January*, 594 x 420 mm, watercolour and ink on watercolour paper, 2014
Source: Courtesy of the artist, Lisa O'Brien

On the other hand the forest can be a sanctuary. In Primo Levi's book *If Not Now, When?* (2000), the Polessian forest-swamps double as a place of potential danger but also as somewhere to shelter and hide. Russian, Polish and Jewish partisans are trapped behind enemy lines and travelling on foot across Eastern Europe during the Second World War. They are grieving for lost family and ways of life, they are homeless, outcast, hunted and the forest is a temporary home and hiding place. The artist Anselm Kiefer also references the forest in his work as both refuge and a place of fear for his family during this same period (Gayford, 2014). From Kiefer and Levi's work I got a sense that the forest is a place beyond the law.

In very large, dense wild forests it can feel as if human authority is suspended. The forest has its own order related to its survival; trees re-seed and natural clearing takes place through the decay and teeming wildlife all perfectly functioning as an ecosystem. The forests existed and survived before humans after all. They provide a connection with a time that is very remote to us, in another, pre-human era. When humans are brought into the picture there is also the realisation that this release from human order could pave the way for a greater freedom of creativity.

'A sylvan fringe of darkness defined the limits of Western civilization's cultivation, the margins of its cities, the boundaries of its institutional domain; but also the extravagance of its imagination' (Pogue Harrison, 1992, p. ix). The edge of the forest is intriguing. It is the cusp of a different world. The device of the wardrobe portal (made from a magical apple tree) in C. S. Lewis's books emphasises that. It is a literal doorway into the otherworldliness of the forest. On the other side the potential for the imagination is boundless. We step into a mythical magical world, full of history, the atmosphere retaining imprinted memories of events gone by, of life and death, murder and fear, light and wonder. 'To enter a wood is to pass into a different world in which we ourselves are transformed' (Deakin, 2008, p. x).

How can we as artists engage with this history, mythology, and monumental physicality and distil it into an artistic response? It seems an overwhelming task. As Robert Macfarlane says 'Wildness is not only a property of land – it is also a quality which can settle on a place with a snowfall or with close of day' (2008, p. 193). So when considering an artistic response it is perhaps important to focus on that quality of wildness, of remoteness, and how it feels to me.

REFERENCES

Deakin, Roger (2008) *Wildwood: A Journey Through Trees*. London: Penguin.

Gayford, Martin (2014) 'Anselm's Alchemy', *RA magazine*, Autumn, 22 September. Available online: https://www.royalacademy.org.uk/article/anselms-alchemy [Accessed 4 Dec 2014].

Levi, Primo (2000) *If Not Now, When?* London: Penguin.

Macfarlane, Robert (2008) *The Wild Places*. London: Granta.

Pogue Harrison, Robert (1992) *Forests: The Shadow of Civilisation*. London: University of Chicago Press.

Zolkos, Magdalena (2011) 'Violent Affects: Nature and the feminine in Lars Von Trier's *Antichrist*', *Parrhesia*, 13, pp. 177–89. Available online: http://parrhesiajournal.org/parrhesia13/parrhesia13_zolkos.pdf [Accessed 4 Dec 2014].

Composing with Place

Kirsteen Davidson Kelly

Fig. 27   Upright Piano, Glen Nevis, 2014
Source: London Fieldworks

As a pianist working predominantly within the Western art music tradition, I usually perform music that has first been imagined by someone else. I sometimes collaborate with composers as pieces are developed, rehearsed and recorded, and have varying degrees of input into how certain aspects of a piece are shaped. But in almost every case, the composer both generates the ideas and has the final say. My job is to internalise the composer's intention, to make the ideas feel like my own, to combine our voices. This process often requires me to walk a thin (and intriguing) line between doing precisely what I am told and feeling free to do as I like.

For *Remote Performances*, I wanted to explore ways to imagine and create music collaboratively with local people, working in response to the surrounding environment. I chose to work with people who have musical backgrounds but who don't consider themselves to be composers, so that we could develop processes together and generate work that could not exist without our respective inputs. I spent three days working with two people who live locally – shipwright Charlie Menzies and music lecturer Miriam Iorwerth.

COMPOSITION 1 – CHARLIE MENZIES

We began our collaboration by walking through Glen Nevis in glorious sunshine, stopping at a beautiful spot where we sat on a long flat rock and talked for a while. Charlie took out his fiddle and played a couple of tunes. I asked him to improvise, looking up the glen towards the hills, and videoed his playing. Back at Lochaber College we reviewed the video. Charlie identified six short motifs from his improvisation in the glen, and I began playing them on the piano, not adding much beyond a couple of bass notes, and improvising several performances that wove the different motifs together. At this point we hadn't defined a structure, but two days later Charlie came back with a poem, written during one of his 'wilderness journeys' some time before, that he felt had been waiting for this music. We decided to incorporate the poem into the performance.

> *My soul's song had a touch of sadness, disconnection, there were no raptors,*
> *my shadow, my mountain mentor, the raven was not there!*
> *I was truly alone.*
> *(Charlie Menzies, from 'Bumble Bees in the Broom')*

The six musical motifs were labelled according to elements that appear in the poem – clover, bumblebees, soul, shadow, river, parents. We worked these motifs around the phrases of the poem, allowing for a degree of flexibility in performance – some of the motifs occur at fixed points in the text, others are selected in the moment in response to Charlie's reading of the poem.

COMPOSITION 2 – MIRIAM IORWERTH

Miriam and I spent a morning at *Outlandia* and in the woods around, discussing and photographing textures in the landscape. Miriam focused on three views for her composition. Trees seen from the hut, light green, growing close together but with space and light between, moving gently in the breeze. Moss by the boardwalk, spongy, with ferns growing through it like fingers. And, by the path, straight, bare-trunked trees with dry, purple-tinged ground beneath. Miriam wanted to write a piece that captured a sense of being in the place at one moment in time, and we worked directly from these three images to develop musical ideas at the piano. She

Fig. 28
Composition 2, extract, performed by Kirsteen Davidson Kelly in Glen Nevis, 2014
Source:
Miriam Iorwerth and Kirsteen Davidson Kelly

specifically wanted to use non-melodic material, so we worked from the textures in each of the photographed images. Miriam described the kind of tonality she imagined, and I played groups of notes (pitch sets) in different parts of the keyboard (registers) until she heard what she wanted. Once we had defined the pitch set and register for each image, short musical motifs emerged very easily. I improvised and Miriam made further suggestions and revisions. The resulting piece consists of four sections based on the images: swaying trees, moss, swaying trees again, and finally the straight, bare-trunked trees with dry ground beneath.

Being in the landscape together informed the composition and the performance of both pieces in a way that I hadn't experienced before. Spending time with Charlie and Miriam in Glen Nevis seemed to give me a visceral sense of what they wanted to say musically. The performances took place in the forest below *Outlandia* among the straight, bare-trunked trees that inspired the final section of Miriam's piece, on a piano, slightly de-tuned through its relocation, that produced a rather ethereal effect.

Fig. 29   Charlie Menzies, *Glen Nevis improvisation*, 2014
Source: Kirsteen Davidson Kelly

A Sense of Distance

Lee Patterson

Fig. 30   Lee Patterson, fieldwork in upper Glen Nevis, August 2014
Source: London Fieldworks

From a distance, how can one predict what may be heard in an area without informed, prior knowledge of that location? By pouring over accounts of the area in question? Studying Ordnance Survey maps? Searching satellite images, zooming in to glimpse a pixellated something of interest?

Even though these initial approaches are useful when assessing sound recording possibilities, such research is hampered by an over reliance on visual cues, is limited by representational scale and the information others have chosen to omit. They compound a sense of distance from the desired location and one is left to rely on a kind of remote sonic imagining based on such scant knowledge.

As a result, I approached *Remote Performances* with a collection of loose ideas as to outcome, a suitcase full of sound making devices (none of which were used), sound recording techniques developed over several years in other remote places and a handful of potentially interesting locations marked on my map of Ben Nevis and Fort William.

Given the time available and distances involved, it soon became apparent that some kind of wide ranging sound gathering or survey was an unrealistic end. Equally, making sound with the objects I had brought along was impractical given the space and time needed to set them up, not to mention their total weight in relation to *Outlandia*'s location halfway up a steep valley side, plus this idea didn't engage with the surrounding landscape in a way that I found interesting.

Instead, I opted to focus upon sonic phenomena closer to the projects' focal points of Glen Nevis, the *Outlandia* structure itself and the accommodation at Roshven. Working with the challenges of these locations, this approach yielded a variety of recordings, of which, a good number were either unexpected, or material I wouldn't have predicted to find interesting such as an amusing discussion with passing tourists, the sounds of their vehicles (Glen Nevis gets busy during the summer), or an attempt to align the satellite dish on the day prior to first transmission and the associated bemusement of the Resonance 104.4fm team.

Other recordings were perhaps a little more predictable, though no less interesting – the white noise of local waterfalls, passing thunder and rain, the action of wind upon wire fences and drips or beads of water seeping out of the mountain side onto carefully placed hydrophones. Venturing out onto Loch Ailort with Bruce Gilchrist at the helm of a canoe, offered the rare opportunity to lower in a pair of hydrophones and hear the grunts of cod or pollack amidst the near cacophony of aptly named pistol shrimps. While other sounds came as a complete surprise, such as a bat, inaudible to my ageing ears, echo-locating above 16 kHz and only noticed in the spectrogram of a recording of evening sounds at Roshven (see Plates xxxii–xxxiii).

With reference to various musical forms as well as classic field recording, the best of these sounds were prepared for broadcast by editing and composing, exploring contrasts of volume and texture, sudden shifts in dynamic and the inclusion of certain noisier elements from the collected recordings.

This strategy paid off in an unforeseen fashion when the piece disrupted the act of live transmission in a way I had suspected might be possible but hadn't really expected to happen. During my broadcast the composition streamed from *Outlandia* included recorded sounds of the transmission breaking down. The radio technician in London mis-read this, assuming that he was hearing an actual failure in the satellite link and he temporarily halted the live broadcast. Given my means of production, I was pleasantly surprised.

Notes for a Video

Benedict Drew

Fig. 31 Benedict Drew, fieldwork, Roshven, video still, August 2014
Source: Courtesy of the artist, Benedict Drew, and Matt's Gallery

Plate i Benedict Drew, *Notes for a Video*, digital collage, 2014
Source: Courtesy of the artist, Benedict Drew, and Matt's Gallery

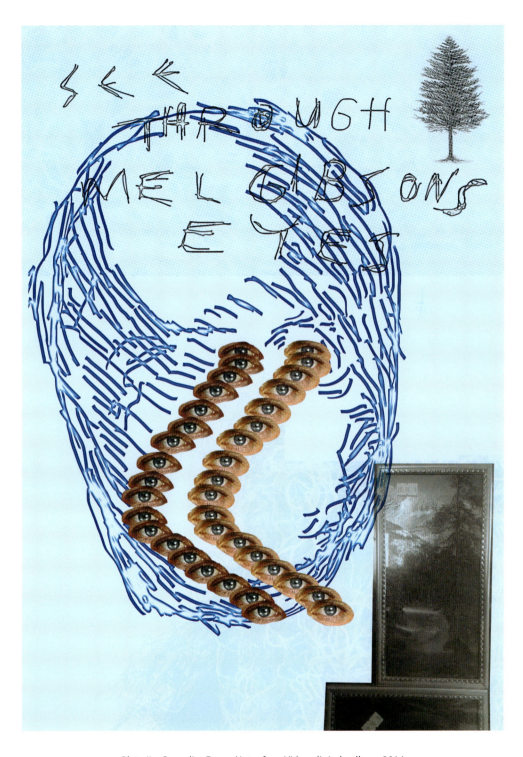

Plate ii Benedict Drew, *Notes for a Video*, digital collage, 2014
Source: Courtesy of the artist, Benedict Drew, and Matt's Gallery

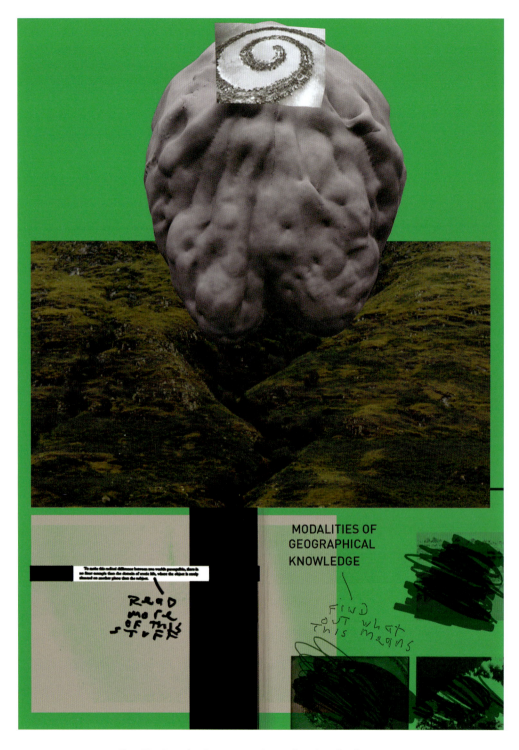

Plate iii Benedict Drew, *Notes for a Video,* digital collage, 2014
Source: Courtesy of the artist, Benedict Drew, and Matt's Gallery

Plate iv Benedict Drew, *Notes for a Video,* digital collage, 2014
Source: Courtesy of the artist, Benedict Drew, and Matt's Gallery

The Contemporary Remote

Bruce Gilchrist

Fig. 32   London Fieldworks, *Polaria* fieldwork, Hold With Hope Peninsula, Northeast Greenland, 2001
Source: London Fieldworks

They rise from the fields like smoke in great, swirling currents, rising higher and spreading wider in the sky than one's field of vision can encompass. One fluid, recurved sweep of ten thousand of them passes through the space within another, counterflying flock; while beyond them lattice after lattice passes, like sliding Japanese walls, until in the whole sky you lose your depth of field and feel as though you are looking up from the floor of the ocean through shoals of fish. (Lopez, 1999, p. 154)

We've been remote. Very remote. For some in our small group the alien nature and forbidding immensity of the looming black basalt cliffs and the ash coloured ribbon of beach we stood on immediately started to unsettle the mind: we have to stay in this barren wilderness for the next month? For me it didn't start off that way. Once we'd touched down, Hold With Hope Peninsula in Northeast Greenland initially appeared to me like a colossal version of a post-industrial wasteland. The colour of the terrain, its black and greyness, the crunch of it underfoot, reminded me of Lanarkshire shale heaps, 'bings' in the Scottish vernacular, that I spent my formative years playing on. It was weirdly familiar. The 'remoteness' became an aspect of scale appearing to my mind through a Lilliputian filter. Nature is anything that hasn't been constructed by the human mind; to say the same about remoteness – that the human mind hasn't constructed it – is problematic since the mind clearly has something to do with it. The human mind continually searches its memory for symbolic associations to whatever it perceives. Even in sleep an external event can become symbolically incorporated into dream content.

Jo's experience on arrival was different: we had arrived in a desert landscape, familiar to her from formative years spent in the Middle East. For her, the feeling of a desert remoteness was compounded looking into the eyes of the animal residents: arctic foxes, terns, muskoxen, who probably hadn't come across anything like us before, had never been 'constrained by the schemes of men' and displayed no fear. It was a remote place through the discernible lack of human presence. The great nature writer and arctic traveller Barry Lopez describes time in the arctic wilderness as a passing animal, and how the creatures there display 'a calming reminder of a more fundamental order'. Through him we were able to imagine being on the edge of what he described as a 'corridor of breath' (Lopez: 1999), part of the planetary network of migration paths, a seasonal animal pulse of great breeding colonies, which in the high arctic last only a few weeks. In the beginning we had 24-hour continual sunshine, a sky full of noisy, fledgling, migratory birds and abundant flora making the most of the brief high arctic summer.

Before we arrived in this relative terra incognita in August 2001, I remember anticipating profound feelings of remoteness from the urban centre that we'd temporarily left behind. But this wasn't immediately actualized on arrival. Perhaps because it seemed so 'busy', with all the wildlife activity. Walking back down the beach to the Twin Otter aircraft, the Danish pilots shouted out to remind us they'd be back to pick us up in a month. Perhaps the proximity to the effort of getting there – the weeks of logistics and days of travelling – and previous consumption of video clips and high-resolution photographs functioned as a buffer against the reality of the moment. The Inmarsat satellite phone stashed in its Pelican case created a safety net, along with the HF radio contact we knew we were about to establish with the Danish Polar Centre after building the antenna. We had a connection to the established Polar network as a result of having to feign being a scientific expedition, in order to leverage the necessary permit to access the protected territory to make our artwork, *Polaria* (Gilchrist and Joelson, 2001).[1]

Shortly after our arrival, the arctic terns disappeared, flying south towards the Antarctic, to environments more conducive to growth and survival, chasing the continuous daylight regime they seem to crave. More devastating, over one day the following week, was the endless gathering and departure of staggering numbers of geese. The geese, like all the other animals seemed to define the place through their presence, but the geese more so because of the sheer number and sound of them. Their sweeping departure south created an immense void that we all agreed was keenly felt. I can still feel the desolate tug of it, and remember the new soundscape: a pervasive uniform slab of unidentifiable atmospheric sound that seemed to bear down on us from even further north.

Animals are keyed-in to environmental cues and leave for good reason. After about three weeks of working, a stunning reversal had gradually set in. The sun was low now, tracking just above the horizon at its lowest point and small icebergs were starting to grind up onto the beach. This was a concern as the beach functioned as the landing strip, our only route out. We started to sense ice particles and sleet carried in the wind and soon after this our guide, a former Sirius dog-sledge patrol veteran, retreated into his tent for days on end as if suffering from a premature winter depression. We became neglectful and compromised our safety: bear alarms weren't tested as often as they should've been and rifles weren't checked every day. The increasing cloud cover and precipitation also incapacitated the solar panels forcing us to break out the generator, a brand new model borrowed during the plane-hop at Mestersvig, a Danish military base in Scoresby Land in the south. It didn't work. But fortunately, using the trickle of power from the solar panels to keep the satellite phone working, we were able to call the Danish Polar Centre to schedule an early pick up by plane. It was while waiting for the return of the Twin Otter and feeling exposed in a window of vulnerability that the remote attained a fresh edge. This was a humbling experience – one that Timothy Morton might describe as a 'humiliating descent towards the Earth' (2010).

The remote had become reframed by the diminished infrastructure and sudden awareness of fragile safety nets. Something I had initially perceived as somewhat out of register – a preconceived notion of remoteness as a strange geographical and psychological dislocation within a social equation – how much one can hack one's own company – became focused through technological dysfunction brought about by a change in the weather. The experience of this project and others like it have been seminal to our reading of the remote as an enigmatic mesh of natural, technological and psychological factors that affect different people in different ways.

The *Syzygy* project in 1999, took us and another small team of people to an unpopulated southern Hebridean island. *Syzygy* preempted the remote, isolation narrative of the Endemol reality TV show *Castaway*. We chose not to utilise a video link-up, instead relying on evolving texts posted daily on a proto-blog where readers could interact, and through an animated sculpture employing a visual language of deep abstraction to translate weather events and physiology transmitted from the island into machine behaviour in the Institute of Contemporary Art gallery in London. *Syzygy* employed remote sensing technologies and computer controlled telecommunication to interrogate mediated experience. The activity on the island was opened up to the possibility of multiple perspectives and interpretations, questioning whether mediation can truly represent an actual event in the mind of the audience. The audience was at liberty to juxtapose one of a number of literary accounts of an event by one of several authors, with a highly abstracted physical representation of the same event. Through the *Syzygy* project, different ideas of the remote were at play: the distance created between the actual source event and the experience of the audience distilled through multiple layers of representation; the geographical separation between audience and event (over 500 miles).

Exploring modes of production and reception have been vital to our practice; *Outlandia* as an ongoing creative experiment that connects an urban centre to its periphery is firmly rooted in that aspect of the practice. *Remote Performances* (2014) enlisted a portable radio broadcast setup, a natural development of the *Outlandia* ethos. *Outlandia* connected to the 'urban centre' through its engagement with local population while the broadcast medium exploded the 'periphery' into a polyphony of centres: nodes in a network linked to clusters of remote listeners.

London Fieldworks' *Outlandia* project has been described in various ways: an artists' fieldstation, a treehouse studio, creative cabin architecture belonging to the tradition of huts and retreats. However valid these descriptions might be we prefer to regard it as a form of performative architecture: that the actuality of the building is largely defined by the acts and performances it elicits from those who choose to engage with it. In this way it can be thought of as an actor within a heterogeneous association of humans and non-human things. *Remote Performances* radically extended *Outlandia*'s heterogeneous associations via a multidisciplinary radio art project in collaboration with Resonance 104.4fm, involving both local people and a diverse range of commissioned artists. *Outlandia*'s off-grid mountain location came with very specific logistical problems including the provision of a reliable temporary electrical power source and the ability to connect with a stable communications network in order to stream live audio to a global audience via the internet and FM radio in London. Electricity was provided via a pair of BOC Hymera portable hydrogen energy generators that ran extremely quietly at 45 decibels and produced water as the only by-product. Connecting with a stable network initially proved more of a challenge. A Tooway satellite system was brought to the site in its component pieces, assembled and then securely anchored to an improvised platform constructed at the base of the cabin's supporting tree. This position would be more stable than mounting it onto the roof of the swaying cabin. The guts of the radio station were plugged into a laptop and router and then cabled several metres to the ground-based antenna below. To establish a connection to the network, the Tooway antenna was fixed in a SSE direction to establish line of sight with the geostationary Eutelsat Ka Sat satellite,[2] 36,000km above the equator. This band of space above the equator is termed the Clarke Belt[3] after *Wireless World* magazine published British Science Fiction author Arthur C. Clarke's 1945 paper, 'Extra-Terrestrial Relays – Can Rocket Stations Give Worldwide Radio Coverage?' (1945). Yes they can as it turns out, but unfortunately for us our initial line of sight and access to the Clarke Belt was blocked by large pine trees nearby. Permissions were sought and granted and a local woodsman was summoned to successfully clear the sight line.

Our oscillatory urban-rural practice has eventually led to questions around the idea of a contemporary remote: is there a new kind of remoteness related to the proliferation of technology and technologically enabled perception that is just as likely to be found in the inner city backstreet or suburban living room as in the High Arctic, a Hebridean island, or Highland glen?

Nature? Whatever it is that has sprung up, whatever has been generated and comes to be. What is a wilderness? It has been suggested that wilderness doesn't in fact exist, that it is an invention of the human imagination, a state of mind. While some regard this as too extreme, it is accepted that wilderness does in fact have to be designated by someone. Society gives wilderness meaning and decides where to put it. Wilderness is a human environment, but not for humans, sometimes with legislation around it to restrict access. Roderick Nash writing about 'Wilderness and the American Mind' (2001) suggests that Anglo-American civilisation created wilderness to counter Western technological culture in the late twentieth century. A social construct.

Thinking about the future can become like a wilderness, and to survive it with any success we need to know what is going to be out there in the new world we are going to have to move through. The contemporary remote is informed by a technological projection of the future, big data analysis interpreted by media pundits and experts conjuring spectres of the near future. As a consequence of this, mainstream society begins to consent to a particular vision of nature as something which we were formerly able to turn to in order to find comfort in its symbolic continuity and dynamic permanence. But now when we reflect on it, it is 'with considerable doubt and hesitancy and uncertainty' (Metzger, 1996, p. 9).

Geological time, the oldest time on earth where the human race and everything it has ever achieved is little more than a glitch. If, in the remote future, some form of human or extra-terrestrial intelligence scans the Earth's geological record they will find 'anthropogenic markers'. These 'markers' will contain plastics that have disintegrated into fine particles, mixed and adhered to sediment, small rocks and organic debris such as shells to form a conglomerate that solidifies over time to become what is now being called plastiglomerate rock. 'Our results indicate that this anthropogenically influenced material has great potential to form a marker horizon of human pollution, signaling the occurrence of the informal Anthropocene epoch' (Corcoran, Moore and Jazvac, 2013, p. 8). The contemporary remote is a watershed defined by juxtapositions and collisions between unimaginably slow things that have been happening and present over geological timescales, and relatively rapid, technologically enabled events.

Fig. 33 Fixed 42 metre UHF parabolic antenna, Eiscat Svalbard Radar, Frontiers 8, 2004
Source: London Fieldworks

'There is no human knowing that is not looking out from where we are, using our senses and our brains, from an anthropocentric perspective' (Chappell, 1997, p. 211). Speculative Realism has countered what it has identified as the Correlationist view, humans and the world inextricably tied together, the one never existing without the other. Things are imagined as aggregations of even smaller things and described as scientific naturalism, or as social relativism where things are constructions of human behaviours and society. There is current thinking that attempts to navigate a path between the two, giving equal attention to all things at all scales while contemplating their nature and inter-relationships as much as how they relate to us. Ian Bogost declares that 'all things exist, yet they do not exist equally', challenging the anthropocentric perspective, calling for an appreciation of 'the multifarious complexity of being amongst all things' whereby 'reality is reaffirmed, and humans are allowed to live within it alongside the sea urchins, kudzu, enchiladas, quasars and Tesla coils' (2012). Coming out of environmental philosophy and posthuman studies, Bogost promotes a mode of thought in which nothing exists any more or less than anything else – a flat ontology, where humans are no longer of central interest.

Barbara Maria Stafford describes how the emergent sciences of the mind are contributing to new ideas that challenge long-held assumptions about identity, how experience of first person presence in the psyche leaks out and becomes dispersed in the details of our surroundings, 'thought is lost in the automatic activity of fastening jewelry, eating leftovers at work, or holding a garbage can lid' (2007, p. 175). It is this view of something decentred, no longer being axial from which everything radiates that is germane to the concept of the contemporary remote.

A primary aspect of the contemporary remote is the ability to discern the invisible by means of technological augmentation to the human senses, and questions the assertion that 'human knowing' is set within the brainpan. The human artifacted world is busily employing its instruments to interrogate everything. The diminutive spacecraft Rosetta spent 10 years travelling at 55,000kmh chasing a comet over 6 billion km away. On reaching it the spacecraft threw itself into the comet's orbit before deploying a lander to cling onto its surface to probe it and relay images back to Earth. People looking at the photographs could almost imagine touching the comet's rough, pitted surface with its whiff of rotten eggs. In contrast to the conventional idea of a detached geographical and psychological remoteness, the contemporary remote creates the appearance of access to places and things through which to engage the imagination. It draws them nearer.

REFERENCES

Bogost, Ian (2012) *Alien Phenomenology: Or What it's Like to be a Thing*. Minneapolis: University of Minnesota Press.

Chappell, T.D.J. (1997) *The Philosophy of the Environment*. Edinburgh: University of Edinburgh Press.

Clarke, Arthur C. (1945) 'Extra-Terrestrial Relays – Can Rocket Stations Give Worldwide Radio Coverage?' Available online: http://lakdiva.org/clarke/1945ww/1945ww_oct_305–308.html [Accessed 10 Dec 2014].

Corcoran, Patricia L.; Moore, Charles J. and Jazvac, Kelly (2013) 'An anthropogenic marker horizon in the future rock record', *GSA Today*, pp. 4–8. Available online: http://www.geosociety.org/gsatoday/archive/24/6/article/i1052–5173–24–6-4.htm [Accessed 10 Dec 2014].

Gilchrist, Bruce and Joelson, Jo, eds. (2001) *London Fieldworks: Syzygy/Polaria*. London: Black Dog.

Lopez, Barry (1999) *Arctic Dreams*. London: Harvill Press.

Metzger, Gustav (1996) *Damaged Nature: Auto-destructive Art*. London: Coracle.

Morton, Timothy (2010) 'Thinking Ecology: The Mesh, the Strange Stranger and the Beautiful Soul', *Collapse: Philosophical Research and Development*, vol. VI, Geo/Philosophy, January, Falmouth: Urbanomic, pp. 265–93.

Nash, Roderick F. (2001) *Wilderness and the American Mind*. New Haven: Yale University Press.

Stafford, Barbara M. (2007) *Echo Objects: The Cognitive Work of Images*. Chicago: The University of Chicago Press.

NOTES

1 The *Polaria* project focuses on an experience of nature, which is both scientific and subjective and is interested in the ways in which we encounter nature phenomenologically. *Polaria* is an artwork that translates objective fieldwork data into an intimate participative experience. Inspired by medical research into the bio-stimulation effects of full-spectrum polarized light, it involved a month-long field trip to Hold With Hope Peninsula in Northeast Greenland in August 2001. We recorded light and physiological data within a continuous 24-hour daylight regime, with its gradual transition towards sunset emphasizing a seasonal as opposed to a diurnal rhythm. The recorded data was subsequently used to create an interactive virtual daylight installation for a touring gallery exhibition. Gallery visitors are regarded as both users and components of the work, being literally electrified by the installation interface in order to trigger representations of arctic light.

2 The six ton Eutelsat Ka Sat satellite was launched on a Proton rocket from Baikonur in Kazakhstan in December 2010, the second European satellite dedicated to delivering broadband internet connections to Europe and the Mediterranean Basin; the first satellite, operated by Avanti operations of London was launched in November. A previous Proton rocket earlier in December 2010 had failed, dumping three Glonass satellite navigation spacecraft in the Pacific Ocean. Once in geostationary orbit, the Ka Sat's spotbeams connected it to a network of ten terrestrial teleports centrally operated by Skylogic in Torino, a collective tributary to the larger body of chopped up data packets flowing through the cables of the internet. A finite operational lifetime means that Ka Sat will be Space Junk by 2024.

3 Launching geostationary satellites into the Clarke Belt is creating a permanent ring of several hundred machines locked in orbit around the planet. Outside of an orbit that would eventually suck them destructively back into our atmosphere, these machines are allowed to die but never decay. Their futures will not be measured by Earthly geological epochs but in the times of planets and stars.

Second Sketch for Ascent and Descent

Ed Baxter

Fig. 34   Tam Dean Burn performing for Ed Baxter's *Second Sketch for Ascent and Descent*, video still, August 2014
Source: Inga Tillere

INTRODUCTION

The radio artwork the Resonance Radio Orchestra realised for *Remote Performances* was entitled *Second Sketch for Ascent and Descent,* part of a long-projected and occasionally abandoned suite. Bits of this have appeared in *The Spiral* (2010), commissioned by Sound and Music and BBC Radio 3's *Cut & Splice: Transmission* festival; and *Suspension of Belief* (2009), made for the Radia project *Intimacy and Distance*. The theme is transparently simple, while the variations on the theme have allowed for incorporating transmission of a five hour rock climb, multiple simultaneous radio platforms, plentiful mobile communications devices, numerous voices, wide instrumentation and a variety of dramatic narrative techniques – bringing into equilibrium many discrete kinds of audio (drama, documentary, found audio objects, quotation, music, noise, etc.). The realm of the radiophonic is the only place this post-expressionist methodology – with its combination of disparate and even contradictory elements – really makes sense. The aesthetic purpose in such works is to explore in real time ('liveness' is important) as many types of sonic experience as possible in the frame offered by radio, although practically the restrictions of deadline, terrain, available material and machinery means that the tendency towards including everything but the kitchen sink is mitigated by logistics (see Plate xxxvi). That was the case in *Outlandia*, where the working day started with a 45 minute drive followed by a half hour hike uphill to the radio studio and where forgetting a lead or plug meant abandoning firm decisions made the night before.

This *Second Sketch* follows a Fibonacci sequence whereby the length of each section is mathematically determined in advance and material cut to length. In sixteen sections, it comes in at 26 minutes 27 seconds – 10 minutes 10 seconds longer than the *First Sketch* (performed in May 2014 as part of Aleksander Kolkowski's installation *The Exponential Horn: In Search of Perfect Sound* at the Science Museum, with Dudley Sutton reading the text). The compositional process is typically slow and proceeds by fits and starts: the emphasis on the *sketch* indicates a lack of time and as usual I was working up until the last minute, discarding dozens of ideas as impractical (drones directing sheep which in turn direct musicians; peanut butter smeared on surfaces to control the movements of pine martens in homage to Greta Alfaro) or simply irrelevant in the circumstances (burying an imaginary local boy band up to their necks in soil and having them deliver a late night serenade to an enthralled but exhausted audience of hikers, mountain rescuers and art world luminaries).

This was not an entirely egomaniacal project: I simply spent more time obsessing about the details than my collaborators. Here, in Glen Nevis, I worked with Resonance 104.4fm colleagues Peter Lanceley (guitar, voice) and Michael Umney (piano), as well as local musicians Charlie Menzies (fiddle) and Miriam Iorwerth (xylophone). Sarah Nicol engineered, so the whole of the small Resonance team was implicated, along with long-time confederate Tam Dean Burn.

Charlie Menzies proved to be a powerfully engaging person: an improbable interview that I conducted with him (on a day fraught with problems in a state of frazzled nerves) revealed someone integrated into the landscape in a way that the torpid, smog-bound Londoner could scarcely imagine. Here was someone in whom a strain of Romanticism emerged not merely resolved but extended and above all *lived*. For a lapsed academic noddie such as myself, this encounter had the impact of a revelation – gentle enough (brain cells still working – sigh of relief) not to knock the stuffing from me, but as palpable and solid as the hills and the eternal waters that I entered only as a dilettante tourist. The distance between us I began to think of in terms of pedestrian effort and swiftly the image of Walking Stewart appeared in my mind (see Symonds, 2004). Had he ever come here? In spirit surely, I thought. And wasn't this the landscape which the hermit Neil Oram asserted was *man-made*? I took all this to suggest that it was legitimate for me to impose my thoughts on the landscape. Legitimate – and perhaps my only option.

At the centre of this radio work is a recording of the sheepdog trial specially conducted for us by Ewen Campbell, the fatalistic choreography of which combined in my mind with the infant plot line of a phantasmagoric play by Jetson Joelson Gilchrist, performed as a post-prandial entertainment for the *Remote Performances* artists a couple of nights before *Second Sketch* was broadcast. Childhood as an idea emerged, or at least took solid shape in our part of the world, only in the early nineteenth century through the writings of Wordsworth and De Quincey, at the same time that they absorbed and distilled the ideas about Nature suggested in the prolix homespun philosophy of Walking Stewart.

Other elements were instinctively and rapidly drawn or thrown together. First, the toing and froing of the various artists as they encountered *Outlandia* and made their own broadcasts, only to disappear a short while later – another dance, observed as if in a time lapse; another plot which segued with the apocalypse of the child's play. The story, such as it is, is brought to life by Tam Dean Burn in an absurdist delineation of pointlessly busy activity – after which everyone is heartlessly destroyed in comicbook fashion. Secondly, a short song (sung by Peter Lanceley) provides a coda suggestive of a certain impotence or incomprehension in the face of the deteriorating global political situation, the background hum of which seemed to me to be unavoidable even in this overwhelmingly imposing landscape. The idea of throwing rocks it contains not only points to entry-level protest across the world, but also references both De Quincey's 'A Sketch from Childhood' (1851) and Walter Marchetti's *Per La Sete Dell'orecchio* (1989).

Each line in the narrative text could be annotated and some of it exists on the level of a private joke. For reasons that are now obscure (I think it arose from a remark by Sarah Nicol about the difference between sheep and dairy farming), the idea of *carnage* emerged among the Resonance team so that when the word appeared one morning in its right and proper place – a local newspaper headline – it reinforced a feeling that one notices articulated in the menacing landscape of Glen Coe and which likewise characterises the realities of the several war zones in which we currently conduct the campaigns that allow us to live so comfortably. These remote performances (in the Middle East and parts of Asia in our time, further afield in our recent imperial history) came to mind in tandem with the definition of Nature formulated by the

Fig. 35 'Plea for Action to End Carnage …', *Lochaber News*, 31 July 2014
Source: Peter Lanceley

proto-Romantic Walking Stewart; as did the suffocating sense of impotence that accompanies any sober contemplation of one's relation to their remoteness.

But why, you ask – suddenly seeing the outline of the kitchen sink perhaps and not entirely convinced by any of this – why does Zal Cleminson appear? Two related reasons. First, he seems to me to articulate in a pure and modest form an extreme gestural vocabulary which has at length come to typify the dominant strand in contemporary culture. His is a fledgling version of cracked over-statement, of apparently superfluous information which emphatically reinforces certain sounds, something bombastic,

Fig. 36 Danger of Death, Glen Nevis, August 2014
Source:
London Fieldworks

sinister, and deliberately lewd. In the early 21st century this exhibitionist streak, once more or less confined to rock music (a shorthand version of which can be stated in the maxim – *Every guitar solo requires you to stick out and waggle your tongue)*, is articulated in numberless examples of what one might term Spectacular Infantilism – most obvious in public art (the narcissistic sculpture of Antony Gormley, the grisly wooden dolls of Artichoke), but in truth informing all aspects of social life (everything that appears on television 'light entertainment' programmes, tabloid newspaper leader columns, the inflexions and body language of the professional political class, etc.). Secondly, because of his role in the Sensational Alex Harvey Band, I had asked Cleminson to perform on top of Arthur's Seat as part of the Radio Orchestra's sound work for NVA's

Speed Of Light, the minimal and almost gesture-free *No Such Object* (Ed Baxter and Chris Weaver, 2012), which used tiny synthesisers controlled by the infinitely subtle movements of the audience. Sadly, he has retired from live performance so this was not to be, but the idea of his incandescent presence interrupting with Fauvist aplomb a more meditative and recalcitrant mood has stuck with me for years. This fleeting reference to him is by way of modest homage and is an attempt to roll back the years to when infatuated corpsing was still uncanny and fun rather than the symptomatic reflex of a thoroughly demoralised culture.

Paranoia lies at the root of such heightened forms of self-projection. Hence in the text the whistling in the forest, hence in the radio artwork the much stranger whistling of the shepherd (the dog's brain is a kind of forest). Asked why his sheep react the way they do to his dog, the shepherd explains: *They are terrified.* The dog meantime has never looked so happy. The shepherd whistles, the dog runs in circles, the sheep trot and stand stock still, frozen. It is tempting to call such things timeless or eternal, but what we really mean is that they arose before we were born and will still go on after our death. The people, the towns, the trees, even the rocks and mountains – all this will one day be worn away. This belief, along with the concomitant fantasy that the world will be over-run by gigantic creatures (the Revenge of Nature), consoles us and allows us to build a hearth here for a night or two.

If all this sounds portentous, when pressed I'd yet have to focus on the modest reach of such activities. *Ascent and Descent* does not imply a conquering of the landscape and in my mind's eye the scale of ambition is at best that of an amateur rock-climber or a tourist riding in a hot air balloon. We spent a lot of time during *Remote Performances* going up paths or coming down them, usually laden with gear. The wall of celebratory post-it notes in the Visitor Centre was as near as I got to the summit of Ben Nevis and it is more in the mood swings concomitant to creative acts – euphoria, depression – that the visualisation of such radio artworks take place. A rhythm is imposed through these swings onto the landscape, which remains implacable, indifferent, forbidding.

REFERENCES

De Quincey, Thomas (1851) 'A Sketch from Childhood' in *The Works of Thomas De Quincey,* volume 17. London: Pickering & Chatto (2002).

Marchetti, Walter (1989) *Per La Sete Dell'orecchio* [CD]. Milan: Cramps Records.

Symonds, Barry (2004) 'Stewart, John (1747–1822)', *Oxford Dictionary of National Biography.*

SECOND SKETCH FOR ASCENT AND DESCENT

Suddenly it's raining again. When Walking Stewart invented Nature in the late eighteenth century, it was on the rebound from both the East India Company and the warlord Hyder Ali, two masters – Top Hat and Turban, if you like – who reappear through time like figures on the stage of a Victorian nursery play. Stewart's Nature was cast in his own image, if *The Roll of a Tennis Ball Through The Moral World* suggests a coherent image to you. An entity trying to renounce the gravitational pull of the civilised world, an omoousiast, Nature's only child. Though as I've said, it was him was the father – long beard, britches, stout walking shoes – rather than the screaming infant crapping its nappy on emerging into this green void.

On his way north, he was thinking that someone should write and publish a tract denouncing the practice of hostelries providing damp sheets. He was a practical fellow: no one's saying he didn't serve both masters well. Still, both wanted him dead.

And then!?

And then the characters all come together in a forest. Some of them walk up the hill. Some of them walk down the hill. The characters all arrive at different times. One of the characters doesn't show up, in fact never shows up. Some of the characters go, others arrive in their place. Characters engage in a variety of acts: they preserve things, they destroy other things. They are better at destroying than preserving, as a general rule. They don't want to disappoint audience expectations. Some throw their voices into the forest: sound comes back (it's *exactly* as Freud said!). Some stay silent in the forest … not clear what they are doing at this point … but the forest makes sounds of its own, sounds that don't have anything to do with the characters, no matter what they think. Characters engage in a variety of other acts: they move through space, they stay still, they move objects through space too; they leave objects – some objects they leave deliberately, others accidentally, others they leave forever.

And then the characters all leave the forest. Now they gather together in a house. Characters engage in a variety of other acts: they wash, they eat, they sleep, they wash again. Some characters go out of the house and others stay inside the house. The characters open doors, close doors, sit down, stand up, go upstairs, come downstairs. One or two of the characters go into a body of water adjacent to the house, come out again, dry themselves off, go back inside the house. Characters get caught in the rain if they go outside but stay dry if they remain inside. Some characters stay together in small groups of characters. Other characters are more solitary, but mostly characters circle one another, come together briefly, go off and do whatever task they chose to do, come back into one another's orbits, then move on to do another task – chosen or dictated by one of the other characters; by more than one of the characters; or, in some instances, seemingly by all or most of the characters at once.

And then yet more of the characters disappear, and this time only a few are replaced. Until at last all of *our* characters – as we've grown to think of them by now – are gone, none seem to be left. But other characters appear, the same but different. They move this way and that, and you're left with the impression that there is more of this to come.

And then!? …

And then the characters are cast into darkness. Hands of flame surround them. One is transformed into a giant wren, big as a munro, too big to get off the ground – but the din it makes, the din! One is thrown from a fast moving steam train, disappears in a billowing cloud of boiling hot vapour. Another is cast by an unseen hand from a high tree, is impaled on the merciless spikes of its immense branches – there's blood everywhere, eyeballs and intestines and some sort of goo that comes from inside the body and gets everywhere. One explodes from the inside, having consumed an innocuous looking fruit, and not only is the explosion loud enough to shatter all the windows for miles around, the acidic quality of the fruit's flesh – as it rains down in a shower of shattered body parts – is corrosive enough to strip the paint from a fleet of hire-vehicles. And then another, who tries to make a desperate getaway down a boggy track, is attacked by gigantic insects which descend at impossible speed from the sky and of course chew their way through human flesh in next to no time, so that there's not even a scrap of the high-viz yellow waistcoat left over to act as witness to the unspeakable carnage!

And then, as in a dream, the nightmare clown face of Zal Cleminson – fifty times life size, like some lunatic's vision of a hellish disco ball – appears in the locked room where the characters have foolishly sought refuge; and his tongue extends horribly and wiggles more horribly still – eyes rolling, eyebrows dancing lewdly, and with that frightening curly corkscrew red seventies hair style. All the efforts they made earlier, the characters – they take a back seat, pretty much. It's all they can do to evade the terrible fate that seems destined to befall them. They zigzag in the encroaching gloom, bumbling this way and that, only to fall into bottomless pits where dragonfly larvae the size of buses eye them curiously for an instant before gobbling them whole; or to plunge down a rocky crevice that suddenly appears from nowhere, tumbling down unbearably sharp stones which rip their clothing to shreds – so that when they at last come to a halt, they are naked as the day they were born … only to die in horrible agony in the jaws of an enormous bear. Others flee through the trees, where they breathe their last in the steely, sticky webs of colossal black and blue spiders whose poisonous jaws drip primordial ichor and whose twitching legs probe their immobilised victims with icy curiosity.

The Top Hat and the Turban look on at all this, exchange words we cannot hear; but clearly they are in some strange way directing the action now, in charge perhaps – though how can that be when they are clearly characters themselves, even distinct characters? Still, their bearing is such that they are clearly unafraid that anything will happen to them. This immunity lends them a certain grandeur which we might call timeless, so that the very meanness of their figures – the pale skinny one in the top hat and tails, the darker tubby one in the turban and robes – simply doesn't occur to us. They seemingly provide a still centre or at least a sense of continuity that all this other bombastic stuff lacks.

And then other things happen – are happening – 'off stage', as it were. But bear in mind no one has suggested this *is* a stage: far from it, nothing could be more solid, more real, than the landscapes – the forest, the hill – and the environments – the house, paths, infrastructure, what not – where this all takes place.

If we try to listen, we can just hear these things, this activity, which we fancy takes place in stillness, in darkness, in a forest, amidst the trees, the spaces in the forest, where we whistle – whistle and listen to our own whistling, and fancy we have a place here and a role.

Wrapped in a damp bedsheet, the wind roaring, I lay waiting for the dawn – which rose slowly, stealthily; and then I was on my way.

> *I threw a rock into the ocean*
> *ocean with its back to me*
> *so slow the motion of the tide*
> *it took an eon to retreat*
> *I threw a rock into the ocean*
> *ocean with its back to me*
> *on the other side of earth*
> *they were dropping bombs for me*
> *I threw a rock into the ocean*
> *ocean with its back to me*
> *on the other side of earth*
> *they were making shoes for me*
> *I threw a rock into the ocean*
> *ocean with its back to me*
> *on the other side of earth*
> *they were singing songs for me*
> *I threw a rock into the ocean*
> *ocean with its back to me*
> *so slow the motion of the tide*
> *it took forever to retreat*

Did you get what you wanted? Yeah, yeah, think so – lots of it.

Euphonium at Sea

Sarah Kenchington

Fig. 37   Sarah Kenchington, Loch Ailort, August 2014
Source: London Fieldworks

I thought I would use my time at *Outlandia* to continue with some experiments I had been doing with brass instruments and water. I had pictured all this happening up a mountain, sitting in a cave, with water from a nearby stream trickling into my euphonium. It wasn't like that. I climbed to the tree house, got really puffed out and didn't want to go up the mountain again. Luckily we were staying by the sea, so I thought I would do something there. One of the good things about being geographically remote, for me, is about having limited choices, having to be resourceful, to work with what is available. It is a shift in perspective, it is not necessarily a place that is organised for our convenience, it's not all about us, I like that. It's a thing I have struggled with as a music performer, how to make it not about me and what I can do. It is central to the reason that I adapt and build my own instruments. It is an attempt to shift the focus. I like to make it so that what the instruments do, comes from something other than me. In that way, the word remote also says something about my relationship with my instruments when I am playing them.

By letting the instrument do its thing, external physical forces get involved in shaping the music. The euphonium I brought with me to *Outlandia* was part of a brass band I have been developing. I use conventional brass instruments that are adapted to be played with a foot pump, rubber inner tube, and a balloon membrane stretched over the mouth piece. This makes the horns playable over a much wider register and longer duration than normal. They are also incredibly unstable and almost impossible to dictate to. This is typical of my interventions. There is something a bit punk about what I do. Sometimes I feel like I am vandalising finely honed pieces of equipment. Musical instruments are designed, over many generations, to be predictable, they are the tools of an orderly collaboration of musicians. Great lengths have been gone to, to make these objects tuneable, the tones, stable and balanced, the ergonomics designed so they can be played with virtuosity. My instruments have all these qualities undone. They often can't be tuned, they behave unpredictably and are no longer at all easy to play in a conventional sense. On top of all that I may do something to further hinder progress, to attempt to play more than one instrument at a time or to bring in another influence or driving force to the music, often harnessing the unpredictable nature of fluid or air flow dynamics, gravity, friction and latent energy converted through mechanical devices.

When I first took my bag of bits down to the shore at Lochailort, the evening was calm and the sea was lapping in and out of the rock pools in an orderly and soothing manner, it was a tranquil scene. I connected up the foot pump, inner tube and valves to the euphonium, then dunked it in the water. I found a place where the horn was at just the right level so it was filling and emptying with the waves, and so that the balloon membrane was being intermittently submerged. I pumped up the inner tube and started to play. When the water went in the horn the sound was stifled, as it was emptying it bubbled a beat, and when the balloon submerged a deep bass undertone emerged. I changed the note occasionally but mostly I just listened to what was coming out. The sound was like a beach party heard from inside someone's body, or like a trumpet drowning and being sick. I

liked the visceral quality of it. Over the next few days I continued my experiments. The sea got choppy, I found a huge pipe on the beach, I stretched a rubber glove over one end and pumped air through it, and it sounded like African drumming and a sewing machine mixed together, I don't know why. Then I tried attaching one end of the pipe to the euphonium, and putting the other end in the sea. I imagined I was talking to the whales, I probably was (see Plates xxiv–xxv).

Fig. 38 Sarah Kenchington, Sea Euphonium, Loch Ailort, August 2014
Source:
London Fieldworks

A few weeks later I went to the Isle of Eigg, another remote location, to continue the experiments. I wanted to do something in the sea, but on my way to the beach I heard a strange watery rhythm coming from a bush. It was a pump, submerged in a tank of water. (On Eigg they use hydraulic ram pumps to get the water up the hill from the spring to the high crofts.) I dunked my horn into the water tank, the same way I had done in the sea, and played along with the rhythm of the pump. It sounded like voices, like dirty cartoon farting rap music. The rhythm was persistent but not quite solid, that was the most important thing, to hear the imperfections. I think the turbulence of the bubbles coming out of my horn where effecting the pace of the pump, it was like a proper jam. I was alone but it didn't feel like I was the only one playing.

Hydram pumps are amazing mechanical devices that are powered by the gravity of falling water. The water falls through valves that intermittently open and close. Like the valves in your heart, it is an arrangement that converts a steady flow of fluid into an audible rhythm. The principle that governs this behaviour is very similar to the conditions that create sound. It is a to and fro of equally opposing forces, a steady but not stagnant state. The water pushes a valve open then the valve pushes back over and over. It is the same thing you can see happening when you play a horn with a balloon membrane, the air pushes past the balloon then the balloon snaps shut, the resulting vibration is what you hear as sound. It's what it's all about.

I don't know if you go to somewhere remote to get away from yourself or to get back to yourself, to detach or to reattach. My feeling is it may be to do with finding a place where you can become aware of the pulse, the to and fro between opposing forces. All I know is the less control I had over the sounds my instruments were making, the more human they seemed to become. It made me aware that the forces that governed the flow of water in a pump or the coming and going of the waves in the outside world, were the same as the ones sloshing around inside us all.

Notes After a Week of Wandering

Bram Thomas Arnold

Fig. 39   *Throwing Rocks at Trees*, performance still, *Remote Performances*, Glen Nevis, Scotland, August 2014
Source: Courtesy of the artist, Bram Thomas Arnold

I.

nature /na-cher/ n (often with *cap*) the power that creates and regulates the world; all the natural phenomena created by this power, including plants, animals, landscape etc. as distinct from people; the power of growth; the established order of things; the cosmos; the external world, *esp as untouched by man* [...] (*Chambers Dictionary*, 2006, p. 1004) (that last italicization is mine).

II.

The trouble with language is that it is the first barrier between oneself and the world. One can also however imagine language as a bridge, the only way off the small island of one's consciousness and out, into that swirling mass of world. The trouble is as soon as you label something, as you do with language, you inherently label it as something other, something over there, something not me, something else.

III.

Actions For And Against Nature, whilst initially conceived as a way of crossing this bridge, is really about pointing at all these labels we have created and screaming 'THERE IS NO GAP BETWIXT US!' It's a part of me, and it's a part of you, and it's a part of that grass blade and it's a part of that tree, a part of that building, and that town hall. The *Actions* are for ecology, and against the term *Nature*, pointing at its problems and the problems it has caused us.

IV.

Nature. The word hangs before us, an immediate separate entity that we then entrench with an almost endless series of synonyms and linguistic pirouettes: countryside, wildness, wilderness, *The Great Outdoors*, we further elaborate and name all the things within it from rocks to books, trees to brooks. Nature, as discussed by Timothy Morton is a great metonymic phrase that we have forgotten we are part of and Morton ' ... argues that the very idea of "nature" which so many hold dear will have to wither away in an "ecological" state of human society' (2007, p. 1).[1]

When you are physically there with it though, feet touching earth, pinned to mud by gravity, you are part of it, as Jackson Pollock once said in answer to a question: ' ... I am nature' (Seckler, 1964).[2] The atoms on your fingertips mingle with the feather you're holding, you are entwined and deeply involved, you are together, one, there is no barrier, no bridge. The case for ecology without nature is about trying to make us aware that the bridge off each of our islands was not built by us. It is neither a separate entity nor a separating force, it is more akin to a

Plate v View from *Outlandia*, 2014
Source: Inga Tillere.

Plate vi *Outlandia*, 2013
Source: Luke Allan.

Plate vii *Outlandia (interior)*, 2010
Source: London Fieldworks.

Plate viii *Outlandia*, 2010
Source: London Fieldworks.

Plate ix *Outlandia* boardwalk, 2014
Source: Inga Tillere.

Plate x Understory, 2014
Source: Inga Tillere.

Plate xi Start of the *Outlandia* boardwalk, 2013
Source: Luke Allan.

Plate xii   Ingrid Henderson en route to *Outlandia*, 2014
Source: London Fieldworks.

Plate xiii *Local Spot* broadcast: Ingrid Henderson, 5 August 2014. 'Harpers were around in the Clan system, 300 years ago. Every Clan Chief had a piper, a bard, and a harper and we were really important. No music was written down; it was all passed down orally. As the Clan system started to die out harping was virtually lost. I'm playing a Clan Macdonald melody from 1614'
Source: Inga Tillere.

Plate xiv *Local Spot* broadcast: Cèilidh Trailers, 4 August 2014. 'A Cèilidh is a gathering of folk who know they are going to dance. We've fair packed in the gigs from Mallaig to the Commonwealth Games in Glasgow'
Source: Inga Tillere.

Plate xv *Local Spot* broadcast: Isabel Campbell and Ian McColl, 6 August 2014. Ian: 'My father came as a shepherd to the upper reaches in Glen Nevis in 1939 when I was four. The hills were full of sheep. Sadly it's changed completely. There's very little stock in the hills now. They look to me so lonely. If you were well off you had a bicycle to get to town, once a week messages were delivered, a roadman filled potholes in the road'. Isabel: 'In 40 years of living here this is the first time I've been up the Peat Track. My first impression is of the breathtaking scenery across Glen Nevis from the top of this hill. In the old days we had cattle but not tourists. We used to let the cows out on the roadsides to trim the verges in the summertime. You can't let the cattle out on common grazing anymore'
Source: Inga Tillere.

Plate xvi *Local Spot* broadcast: John Hutchison, 8 August 2014. 'The John Muir Trust doesn't use the term "wilderness" but rather wildland and wild places, which could be in a park or a city. In Scotland we own nine estates, including the top of Ben Nevis, although I subscribe to the refrain from the Dougie MacLean song: "You cannot own the land, the land owns you"'
Source: Inga Tillere.

Plate xvii *Local Spot* broadcast: Alex Gillespie, 7 August 2014. : 'We moved up here in 1965 to work at the paper mill and the volunteer mountain rescue team was short of people. There was a recruiting drive and I found myself on the end of a rope… Most accidents resulted from bad navigation. It becomes a big mountain when you are lost. There are at least two people that we've never found'
Source: Inga Tillere.

Plate xviii *Local Spot* broadcast: Willie Anderson, 7 August 2014. 'I was coming up from Edinburgh since I was 13 climbing and moved here in 1969 to work in the pulp mill and joined the rescue team. If somebody's in trouble you help them. I like to think if I'm in trouble someone will come out for me. In the early days we had radios that didn't work. Stones thrown up at windows to call out the team worked instead. We've upgraded ourselves a bit now'
Source: Inga Tillere.

Plate xix *Local Spot* broadcast: Emma Nicholson, 8 August 2014. 'Atlas Arts is "without walls" – we are blessed with not having a venue, and instead working in collaboration with the community and others, focussing on beyond the gallery. I think the "remote" and islands get fetishised'
Source: Inga Tillere

Plate xx *Local Spot* broadcast: John Ireland, Forestry Commission Scotland, 4 August 2014. 'An ant nest is a big complex society – like *Game of Thrones*. There are Robber Ants that go and kill a Queen, steal pupae, run slave colonies. They get up to all sorts of shinanigans'. John Ireland and Sarah Nicol looking for Hairy Wood Ants, 2014
Source: London Fieldworks.

synaptic cleft that draws us out into the world, it is not there as a separate 'thing' at all. We are part of ecology, it is within us and around us, in our streets and homes, in the cities we've built and the industrial wastelands we've walked away from.

V.

My work has burrowed myself into the web of arguments and propositions offered by quantum physics.[3] The lack of constancy of things, at the quantum level, has left me with so little certainty that even as an argument is released into the world it is countered and contradicted by my next action, my next phrase, my next move. As I finished *Swearing an Oath to a Scottish Glen* (see Plate xxix), a text that promises almost Tibetan levels of tranquility and peaceful presence …

> *I hereby undertake not to remove from Glen Nevis, nor to mark, deface, nor bring injury to in any way, any tree, brook, stream, stone or animal: to harm neither sentient being nor physical presence residing therein or belonging to its custody. I undertake not to leave in my wake any foreign body, nor kindle hostile fire nor flame within, and not to smoke within the Glen. I promise to obey all the rules of the Glen, to adhere to pathways, and respect the property and prosperity of others therein, to plan ahead and leave no trace behind.*

… I closed the book from which I read the oath and accidentally kill an insect, immediately blackening the oath I have only just finished uttering. Later on I throw rocks at trees, and later on still, a friend asks me, with concern in her voice, 'Do you hit them? Do you harm them?'[4]

VI.

All the while I am shouting from my childhood fear of the dark encroaching pines and their imported, plantation-like presence. Their socio-political cause, the disaster of these pine trees on these hillsides. And yet I know full well, as Thomas Wolfe, author of the American dream, put it, 'you can't go home again' (1939),[5] that conservation is a flawed project, that it is really a conversation; for to which 'natural state' do you wish to return?[6]

VII.

'I hate these pine trees, I hate 'em'. And I do, and I don't. They make comfortable, quiet, dry spots for wild camping, a nest of needles in dark nooks, they are most entertaining to cycle through on a mountain bike. And yet, from a distant hillside, with their deep straight lines, I can't help but be reminded of troops aligned for battle, or of colonial cartographers, divvying up Africa with a ruler and a setsquare.

VIII.

Poetry. A way of wrapping the bridge, between the self and the world out there where nature supposedly is, in wry jokes and opaque riddles, and beauty, binding us to it and the beyond in knots of words that drip with incongruous honey. It is the Romantic in me who finally found time after *Reading Poetry to Rocks*, to climb a hill away and alone, to serenade the sky with half remembered lyrics from my favourite obscure pop songs. 'A bird you would have loved brought the sky down, but it was worthless to hear it without you around … ' or 'say what you will, but you should understand there are things in this world, that you can't understand, not in a million years … '.[7] All this could only happen after walking, clearing the mind, falling in a bog up to my thighs and dropping my digital recorder in a stream so that of this act, precisely nothing remains.

Fig. 40 *Reading Particle Physics to a River*, performance still, *Remote Performances*, Glen Nevis, Scotland, August. 2014 Source: Courtesy of the artist, Bram Thomas Arnold and Louise Emslie

IX.

The *Actions* are Romantic, and yet the *Actions* are also conceptual. They are linguistically restrained in their titles: each *Action (A)* having to be followed by a form of *content (C)*, an instruction that is *directive (D)* and a *subject (S)* upon which this sequence can be enacted. But after a walk, and a day and a night on a mountainside at the end of a week spent in the Glen being too busy to look at it, new *Actions* announced themselves and took place, just between me and nature in a series of moments that were filled with contradiction and futility and yet somehow found

space for hope. I blew raspberries at the bog which claimed me thigh deep whilst in between shouting profanities at it ('YOU CALL YOURSELF A BOG!! IA'VE SEEN BOGS THA' COUL' SWALLO' A HOUSE! UPTA MA THIGHS, YOU'RE PATHETIC … '), and I said hello to the high heather moors, whispering sweet nothings to them and their bees high on the flanks of An Gearanach in the so called *Ring of Steall*.

Fig. 41 *Reading Poetry to a Rock*, performance still, *Remote Performances*, Glen Nevis, Scotland, August 2014
Source: Courtesy of the artist, Bram Thomas Arnold

X.

This melding, of Romantic disposition with Conceptual restriction, has been uncovered by Jorg Heiser in the work of Bas Jan Ader and a collection of other artists brought together in 2007 in an exhibition called *Romantic Conceptualism*. Heiser defines Romantic Conceptualism as holding an 'interesting tension: using particularly few aesthetic interventions or conceptual instructions, it opens up a particularly large number of possibilities for thinking beyond this choice' (2007, p. 149).[8] The foundations of *Actions For and Against Nature* are bound up in this quote. The *Actions* that took place in Scotland are the start of a series that is as endless as the metonymic environment we continue to create around us and live in: the *Actions* will continue, probing the cleft, finding a way to cross the bridge, screaming at the thing whilst falling in love with it, until *Nature* is renounced and *Ecology* embraced.

NOTES

1   All of Timothy Morton's writing can be seen to build on this one footstep at the beginning of his work *Ecology Without Nature* (2007). See also *The Ecological Thought* (2010), and his most recent work *Hyperobjects: Philosophy and Ecology after the End of the World* (2013).

2   The question was 'Why don't you paint more from nature?' It is recalled by his wife Lee Krasner in a conversation (Seckler, 1964).

3   I must confess I have not spent years in a library mulling over the intricacies of Quantum Mechanics, much of my understanding of the subject is provided by John Polkinghorne in his work for Oxford University Press's Very Short Introduction series (2002). It is the role of the amateur attempting to understand a subject from the outside here that is of interest to me, that 'the powerful play goes on, and you may contribute a verse' as Walt Whitman put it (2002).

4   It is a curious thing acknowledging that you are setting out to explicitly do harm to something, even though the very way we live in the world in Western society implicitly requires us to do harm to our environment quite a lot of the time. Confronting these unacknowledged discomforts in a quasi-slapstick way is one of the jobs of the *Actions* as I see them.

5   I own a copy of Thomas Wolfe's *The Web and the Rock* (1939) that I have locked inside a sculpture that will only be opened at the final showing of work from my ongoing research project *Walking Home* to take place sometime in 2015. The last line of the novel reads 'You can't go home again' which itself became the title for Wolfe's last novel published posthumously. The last page of this novel, with the rest of the text blacked out was shown at a solo show in London in 2009 before I set out to walk from London to the house I was born into, near St. Gallen in Switzerland.

6   Here I am thinking of certain conservation projects in New Zealand that I explored whilst living there in 2004. The successful eradication of rodent pests on Matiu Island in Wellington Harbour has meant the island has become a refuge for non-native as well as native birds for whom it is a haven, however the more aggressive non-native birds were overpowering the native population forcing the conservationists to eradicate them through injecting their eggs during the breeding season.

7   *Serenading the Sky* is an *Action* that is yet to be fully resolved, these two lyric fragments are from *Raja Vocative* by The Mountain Goats, and *Day* by Tamela Glenn respectively. The lyrics from Tamela Glenn are mis-quoted as I remembered them, or interpreted them for the sky, the actual recording is: 'say what you will, but you should understand, there are things that you say, that she won't understand' (1990). Misinterpretation, what you choose to remember, what you choose to forget are the foundations of my practice, and are nowhere more apparent than in this misremembered song lyric, sung to the sky in the dying light of an August day in 2014.

8   *Romantic Conceptualism* curated by Jorg Heiser was an exhibition at Bawag PSK Gallery in Vienna, 2007. Work included that of Ader, alongside Susan Hiller, Tacita Dean, Douglas Huebler and others. An exhibition catalogue with extensive essays was also published.

REFERENCES

(2006) *Chambers Dictionary*, 10th edition. London: Chambers.

Glenn, Tamela (1990) *What Else Do You Do?* [CD]. New York: Shimmydisc034.

Heiser, Jorg (2007) *Romantic Conceptualism*. Bielefeld: Kerber Verlag.

Morton, Timothy (2009) *Ecology Without Nature: Rethinking Environmental Aesthetics.* Cambridge, Mass. and London: Harvard University Press.

Morton, Timothy (2010) *The Ecological Thought.* Cambridge, Mass. and London: Harvard University Press.

Morton, Timothy (2013) *Hyperobjects: Philosophy and Ecology after the End of the World*, posthumanities 27. Minneapolis: University of Minnesota Press.

Polkinghorne, John (2002) *Quantum Theory: A Very Short Introduction.* Oxford: Oxford Paperbacks.

Seckler, Dorothy (1964) 'Oral History Interview with Lee Krasner, 1964 Nov. 2–1968 Apr. 11', *Archives of American Art*, Smithsonian Institution. Available at: http://www.aaa.si.edu/collections/interviews/oral-history-interview-lee-krasner-12507 [Accessed: 9 Dec 2014].

Whitman, Walt (2002) 'O Me! O Life!', *Leaves of Grass*. New York: W. W. Norton and Company. First published 1892.

Wolfe, Thomas (1939) *The Web and the Rock*. New York: Joanna Cotler Books.

Echo. Genius Loci

Ruth Barker

Fig. 42   Ruth Barker in *Outlandia*, August 2014
Source: Inga Tillere

I am an Echo. Above the earth below the sky, caught in the pines like a bag on a bough, rustling. You are my pale and perishable lover. Under the ground you lie, bulbous and dormant, poking your yellow head above the soil in spring and nodding nodding, only to crumple, fade, and turn to mulch. Every year I see you bloom and die. We hardly ever touch. You are brief. I am old as stone.

I am Echo.
I am Echo.
I am Echo.
I am Echo.
I am Echo.
I am Echo.
I am Echo.
I am Echo.
I am Echo.

My body opens itself to the land. The land opens itself to my body. My fingers grow into the soil. My throat presses against bark, under rain-laden thighs. Thighs and peat. Skin and soil. Hair and damp earth. Wrists and heather. Breasts and moss. I suckle the land that I am. I am suckled by the cracks between the hills. I cup my lips to the shale and drink. And the water grows fat from my milk. I am wedded, at last.

I am heavy, grown stiff and calcified. My veins are thick with ringing minerals. I am become this place. You flower, briefly, by my pools. I let you.

The glen is full of whispered words, spoken elsewhere and thrown back. The mist is full of absent throats. Yours, perhaps. I am a dream of something. I am un-remembered, as are you. My hands are translucent, and fading. I am a scuff mark, your footprint on wet shingle; who spoke this way before? Where did they go? And as I leave I look over my shoulder, resting my chin on the mountain. I am as wide as skies. Here. The words that make me who I am build me in their mass and weight. I have spent an immortal lifetime swallowing your words, and spitting them back. And no more. No more. More. I am full of your words, too many. I have cut myself loose. My throat is my own and the glottal stops flop without cease, without care, without story. It has taken a long time.

I am Echo. You are a fading bloom by a forgotten waterway. I am lost in the wind. You are growing wild among the wild garlic. I am a voice spread low over the hills. You are a splash of colour in springtime, brief and overlooked. In the soil you may find me whispering, in mushrooms. Your pollen blows across the sound of me. In the night you may find my murmurs in badgers sets, my sighs under the talons of owls. Your lips trumpet in a crenulated O. Utterance is imprinted here, once was, will be. But I am losing my hold. My voice is hoarse, and distant. Echo. Echo.

The beginning. Here am I, thinking. I will collect my thoughts like pansies in the grass.

On structure. On structure.
On the opening of lips,
And of the opening on to, and up:
On plant life walled in plastic;
On the green-cut grass and whining;
On porcelain;
On clay;
On curlews' wooden wings are paired,
Plied trade, and aching welts;
On the lamplit faces, fag-end lighters;
On the belly-sound in the odyssey's needle;
On the tree grown limbs of the halo spaces;
On longing, with its mouse-feet fingernails;
On the cartograph eviscerate, all like lacewings, slipping,
Walking,
Down holes like open throats.
On the outside typewritten insecticidal rainways;
On the sets of terms for cow parsley, clover,
Lending lyric structure to each meadow;
On speech unfolding time, and limping licking tongues;
On the every day of sacred texts, and eating;
Thick bolts; of silence, shorn and mastered.

[pause]

So, I am a dark continent.
So, I am a dark continent. So, the breeze runs over my topography. So, my forests dig their roots into my soil. My springs well up and spill fresh water. My volcanoes erupt. My earthquakes roar. My avalanche. My mudslide. My tornado. The oceans lap at my circumference. The sky arcs over me. I am strata. I am mighty geography. I am geography.

I am geography and I am geomancy. I am the mapping of territories and the eating of soil. I am a contested borderland. I am the soil that roots beneath walls, between picket lines, and barbed wire fences. I am the stone that runs under mountains and the mud that hold rivers to their beds. I am the cornfield and the desert and the machair and the moorland heathers. I am the deciduous woodland and the rainforest and the plantation and the scorched earth and the dump.

So, I am a dark continent. I am limestone and mud, magma and tectonics. I am acres beneath your feet, and my mountains tower vast over your horizon. I dwarf you. Do you wish to know me, now after all these years?

In my belly I hold the past. Dig down into me. Scrape away my topsoil with brushes. Be gentle. Take it grain by grain.

What do you see? Amphora. Coins. Something made of dark metal. Something made of bone.

What do you see? I see a shape in the mud where wood has rotted away. I see the soil a different colour. I see that something has been burnt here.

Dig deeper. Dig deeper. I see things from the past. I see who we were but might not have been and could have been again. I see hundreds of years of things lost and thrown away and broken and soiled. I see the detritus of centuries.

Yes. That's it. Dig softly. Bees and stamens, pollen grains and breezes. What do you have in your mouth, flower? I have mud and blood and clay and spit.

Dig anywhere. Dig anywhere in me. Cut my turf. Stick your spade into my clay. I am bigger than you. You cannot see me. I am my own toes in my own soil. I throw my tongue's clack clack, and catch it in my ear.

Here I am at last. An old old woman with dirt between her teeth, swinging her legs. My knees creak. I feel as old as stone. I read the lines on my own hands. They're thick as rocks, long as faultlines. I am a goddess, old, with wrinkled tights and housecoat. Sticks and stones do make my bones and words come tumbling after. I am Echo, grown old, still lonely, only a voice in the wilderness, calling and calling until I go away, lost in the hollow of a throat. Clack clack, clack clack, and catch it.

MY HANDS ARE SEDIMENTARY

I hear the sound of breathing to the crust's hushed grate; lush crushed prime in the darkness. I push against the marks already made, colubrine inveterate as The First Dilemma.
I snake into the limbs and lungs of chasms, form them, push them out as pin-heads in the table top plateau. My granite face is dusky in the firelight, and I hang from all the days and times of marble.

The earth is layered in a systematic mass. Above the reach of my head, spangled through the split ends of my hair, is the geocorona. About my shoulders are two colures, great imaginary disks that intersect at the poles and dip in an inordinate ellipse toward the crust of my naval. The belly crust is thin, and on it rests the world. It itches, like a scab. Beneath it, my flesh is new, pink and raw, untried and vulnerable still. It peels off:

oxygen O
silicon Si
aluminium Al
iron Fe
calcium Ca
sodium Na
potassium K

magnesium Mg
titanium Ti
hydrogen H
phosphorus P
manganese Mn
sulphur S
carbon C

These elements are my mnemonic, holding traces of my memory intact, as bound descriptors. They are my sloughed skin. My belly-button, sunk in flesh. Below it is the hot and molten core of me. Down deep, all fire and liquid heat.

WHEN I AM IGNEOUS

I will wrap up. I will turn out. I will move through. I will move up. I will stop out. I will shut up. I will bring back. I will take down. I will move along. I will take up. I will stay in. I will turn down. I will turn up. When I am igneous I will heave and split apart the world, vent forth and tear and burn in red and yellow horror splitting the coast and raining fire upon the surf. And the trees will burn to cinders on my skin, and the air will flame to nothing in my nose, and the night will be incinerated, bleached white and dead by hot compression of my hands. And I will laugh, at the cinders in my hair. When I am igneous.

METAMORPHIC

I am Echo, prophetess of cosmic geomancy. I thumb down the sod with my toes. The eating of clays is a lifetime of seeing; a consummation of time and the geoid span.
Limey morsels dry between my lips, choke my teeth and palette, and I swallow them in clotted lumps. I lick away the sediment with a viscous tongue of story. I am old as Grandmother Spider and as long as the sibylline shadow at my feet. I need no-one.
Here I am, Here I am (I am, I am, I am).

I weave, and the clod comes down like something. Grasses matted.
You may see me in a white dress stained by digging, with a mouth the colour of earthworms.
If you were to build me I would be sackcloth and peat stacked on a grate, with my perfume as the scent of the burning.
If you sang me I would be the sound of a spade.
Flower, I miss you.
In the springtime I will germinate. Straining and extending I will root like wild garlic, laying the brick shock of my foundations, feeling the fragrance of my empty cellars taking shape as my walls break the surface. I will stretch my budding roof across the rag of stars.
In the hollow of my front door step I might set a stone, for baking.

IGNEOUS

The sound of a spade slicing the topsoil and hitting buried stone two inches down. The surface is a clay-based aggregate, or perhaps slag from the separation of metal and ore. Picturing: A mind making the sound of this spade, and eyes the colour of the stone.

SLATE

The undulating landscape and its sheep grazed hills do not unwind
but plough the darkened furrows under stones with hands like thunder.
The horses eat slate under the skies, over the earth.

Under the rain we fall together; in the nothing, begun nothing, before nothing.
We look to our own lead filled faces,
our hemp coloured pockets,
and we pull the woollen circumstance like knitting
round the muddy field, our boots slipping in the glutinous clod,
fingers numb and frozen through our thoughts.

PEAT

My voice has always been there. The earth's crust is trembling. My voice, fractured and split, calling the tails of your words back to you. You mishear, or do not hear at all.

The valleys swallow speech like a ricochet booming round the hills. The wild woods we wrote are not so wild as they are spoken. There is a kind of thinking that roots in the fingers to grow in the grasses and the mud. There is a kind of thinking that is silent, and has no words. Did you hear me? Did you think I said something else? Are you still there?

Goddess, I pull my coat around me, and step out into the rain. You have given me this, I think, though you cannot know it. I can smell the bracken and the leaf mould, and some other underlying odour – horsehair perhaps, or sweat. I light a cigarette and walk, my heels slipping in the mud. I keep my hands in my pockets, pushed down with my nails sunk into my palms. It's evening, but the rain has kept the day so dark that there is not much change as the sun begins to set. The path is indistinct and the grass, as it is crushed, bruises shadows at my feet. My cigarette seals my lips, pinking them with faint pressure. I am Echo. I am Echo walking in my land, slipping down my slope, catching my hair on my branch. I am Echo, with a trickle of rain creeping down the neck of my jacket. I am Echo, catching my breath. I am Echo, feeling the creak of wet cotton. I am Echo, with a leak in my boot.

The wood is shining with moisture. A thousand tiny mirrors lie in every raindrop splashed on every leaf. Every puddle offers up the sky in miniature. Every sopping bank is swathed in silver. The reflections seem more vivid than the ground that holds them up. The world seems indistinct and dim, and I must walk and walk. The world smells of breathing vegetation. I can feel the valley inhale, filling its lungs, and then release. I am clogged with wet ground and I walk. This is my way. And I think about your yellow hair and your eyes, about your mouth and your skin. I think about you, and the sounds you make on the breeze and the way your bulbs plug down into the soil. I think about the way you move, the way you nod your head. I realise I am nodding at the thought of you, dipping my neck at the shoulders as I walk.

PEAT

The feeling of peat is a condition of the old.
Peat between your fingers, thick in your nails or your knuckles.
The age of it as it goes to the fire, and the smell; like heavy lace, but sweet.
This is the oldest geomancy, and the longest.

SEDIMENTARY

Packed earth is as dense
Down deep,
Around the soft of eyes and throats,
Around the curves of ears and ankles,
As the lungs of a long held breath.

There is a funerary loss of the tomorrow.

CLAY

Stamping the night's wet notes from their limbs, flattening their hooves on the Earth's fatness, the horses stand, making the dew come and the world turn. I watch them, and they calm me. The day breaks in pools on their flat backs. Their mole soft lips are gentle reservoirs of erosion. The static of their gorse manes prickles the dawn. This forehead, wider than the span of my hand.
The closing of teeth over clipped turf. The turning and the wrench of blind narcissi roots as the sweet bulbs crush against meat muscle tongues. The sleep-raised heads, with rheumy eyes and sunburnt blazes, wait for the morning to burn off the mist.

LIMESTONE

So the life of Echo as a stratified deposit that rises up through the rocks as an aquifer, petrifying her in healing, numbing water.

REMOTE PERFORMANCES IN NATURE AND ARCHITECTURE

So the death of Echo as erosion and decomposition, her torso an agent in the acidity of unconsecrated soil, crumbling as limestone crumbles, finally, under pressure.

So the body of Echo as an understanding of landscape. This small goddess, in wrinkled tights and housecoat, who was turned to stone slowly, from the inside out. Slowly she has grown into the mountains and the world, underpinning them, becoming them, joining them.

BASALT

Back again. In the hot red lick of angry magma, in the slow drip drip of lonesome stone, the words still bounce in unbidden reverberation. In the dull hiss of the trees there are nonsense rhymes that have no end. No end.

Pare the earth. There is blood beneath the soil,
From which things grow, and
Into which things stick their roots and coil

Up out, blood-fed, and still self-loyal;
Pursing, parsing sod to
Pare the earth. There is blood beneath the soil

Which feeds the cheap stems and the royal
Oaks of ages up; so
Pare the earth. There is blood beneath the soil,

It is a kind of blood placenta boil,
Mud-slick, red-black, and protein-full
Into which things stick their roots, and coil

Their tendrils, plump and oiled
With greasy mud
Into which things stick their roots and coil

And coil, drawing puddled, meaty soil
Up to our nostrils. Drink that scent. And
Pare the earth. There is blood beneath the soil,
Into which things stick their roots, and coil.

No end. In the dull hiss of the trees there are nonsense rhymes that have no end. In the hot red lick of angry magma, in the slow drip drip of lonesome stone, the words still bounce in unbidden reverberation. Back again.

indistinct and dim, and I must walk and walk. The world smells of breathing vegetation. I can feel the valley inhale, filling its lungs, and then release. I am clogged with wet ground and I walk. This is my way. And I think about your yellow hair and your eyes, about your mouth and your skin. I think about you, and the sounds you make on the breeze and the way your bulbs plug down into the soil. I think about the way you move, the way you nod your head. I realise I am nodding at the thought of you, dipping my neck at the shoulders as I walk.

PEAT

The feeling of peat is a condition of the old.
Peat between your fingers, thick in your nails or your knuckles.
The age of it as it goes to the fire, and the smell; like heavy lace, but sweet.
This is the oldest geomancy, and the longest.

SEDIMENTARY

Packed earth is as dense
Down deep,
Around the soft of eyes and throats,
Around the curves of ears and ankles,
As the lungs of a long held breath.

There is a funerary loss of the tomorrow.

CLAY

Stamping the night's wet notes from their limbs, flattening their hooves on the Earth's fatness, the horses stand, making the dew come and the world turn. I watch them, and they calm me. The day breaks in pools on their flat backs. Their mole soft lips are gentle reservoirs of erosion. The static of their gorse manes prickles the dawn. This forehead, wider than the span of my hand.
The closing of teeth over clipped turf. The turning and the wrench of blind narcissi roots as the sweet bulbs crush against meat muscle tongues. The sleep-raised heads, with rheumy eyes and sunburnt blazes, wait for the morning to burn off the mist.

LIMESTONE

So the life of Echo as a stratified deposit that rises up through the rocks as an aquifer, petrifying her in healing, numbing water.

So the death of Echo as erosion and decomposition, her torso an agent in the acidity of unconsecrated soil, crumbling as limestone crumbles, finally, under pressure.

So the body of Echo as an understanding of landscape. This small goddess, in wrinkled tights and housecoat, who was turned to stone slowly, from the inside out. Slowly she has grown into the mountains and the world, underpinning them, becoming them, joining them.

BASALT

Back again. In the hot red lick of angry magma, in the slow drip drip of lonesome stone, the words still bounce in unbidden reverberation. In the dull hiss of the trees there are nonsense rhymes that have no end. No end.

Pare the earth. There is blood beneath the soil,
From which things grow, and
Into which things stick their roots and coil

Up out, blood-fed, and still self-loyal;
Pursing, parsing sod to
Pare the earth. There is blood beneath the soil

Which feeds the cheap stems and the royal
Oaks of ages up; so
Pare the earth. There is blood beneath the soil,

It is a kind of blood placenta boil,
Mud-slick, red-black, and protein-full
Into which things stick their roots, and coil

Their tendrils, plump and oiled
With greasy mud
Into which things stick their roots and coil

And coil, drawing puddled, meaty soil
Up to our nostrils. Drink that scent. And
Pare the earth. There is blood beneath the soil,
Into which things stick their roots, and coil.

No end. In the dull hiss of the trees there are nonsense rhymes that have no end. In the hot red lick of angry magma, in the slow drip drip of lonesome stone, the words still bounce in unbidden reverberation. Back again.

BASALT

Slowly she has grown into the mountains and the world, underpinning them, becoming them, joining them. This small goddess, in wrinkled tights and housecoat, who was turned to stone slowly, from the inside out.
So the body of Echo as an understanding of landscape.
So the death of Echo as erosion and decomposition, her torso an agent in the acidity of unconsecrated soil, crumbling as limestone crumbles, finally, under pressure.
So the life of Echo as a stratified deposit that rises up through the rocks as an aquifer, petrifying her in healing, numbing water.

LIMESTONE

The sleep-raised heads, with rheumy eyes and sunburnt blazes, wait for the morning to burn off the mist. The turning and the wrench of blind narcissi roots as the sweet bulbs crush against meat muscle tongues. The closing of teeth over clipped turf. This forehead, wider than the span of my hand. The static of their gorse manes prickles the dawn. Their mole soft lips are gentle reservoirs of erosion. The day breaks in pools on their flat backs. I watch them, and they calm me. Stamping the night's wet notes from their limbs, flattening their hooves on the Earth's fatness, the horses stand, making the dew come and the world turn.

CLAY

There is a funerary loss of the tomorrow.
As the lungs of a long held breath.
Around the curves of ears and ankles,
Around the soft of eyes and throats,
Down deep,
Packed earth is as dense

SEDIMENTARY

This is the oldest geomancy, and the longest.
The age of it as it goes to the fire, and the smell; like heavy lace, but sweet.
Peat between your fingers, thick in your nails or your knuckles.
The feeling of peat is a condition of the old.

PEAT

I realise I am nodding at the thought of you, dipping my neck at the shoulders as I walk. I think about the way you move, the way you nod your head. I think about you, and the sounds you make on the breeze and the way your bulbs plug down into the soil. And I think about your yellow hair and your eyes, about your mouth and your skin. This is my way. I am clogged with wet ground and I walk. The world smells of breathing vegetation. I can feel the valley inhale, filling its lungs, and then release. The world seems indistinct and dim, and I must walk and walk. The reflections seem more vivid than the ground that holds them up. Every sopping bank is swathed in silver. Every puddle offers up the sky in miniature. A thousand tiny mirrors lie in every raindrop splashed on every leaf. The wood is shining with moisture.

I am Echo, with a leak in my boot. I am Echo, feeling the creak of wet cotton. I am Echo, catching my breath. I am Echo, with a trickle of rain creeping down the neck of my jacket. I am Echo walking in my land, slipping down my slope, catching my hair on my branch. I am Echo. My cigarette seals my lips, pinking them with faint pressure. The path is indistinct, and the grass as it is crushed, bruises shadows at my feet. It's evening, but the rain has kept the day so dark that there is not much change as the sun begins to set. I keep my hands in my pockets, pushed down with my nails sunk into my palms. I light a cigarette and walk, my heels slipping in the mud. I can smell the bracken and the leaf mould, and some other underlying odour – horsehair perhaps, or sweat. You have given me this, I think, though you cannot know it. Goddess, I pull my coat around me, and step out into the rain.

Are you still there? Did you think I said something else? Did you hear me? There is a kind of thinking that is silent, and has no words. There is a kind of thinking that roots in the fingers to grow in the grasses and the mud. The wild woods we wrote are not so wild as they are spoken. The valleys swallow speech like a ricochet booming round the hills.

You mishear, or do not hear at all. My voice, fractured and split, calling the tails of your words back to you. My voice has always been there. The earth's crust is trembling.

PEAT

fingers numb and frozen through our thoughts.
round the muddy field, our boots slipping in the glutinous clod,
and we pull the woollen circumstance like knitting
our hemp coloured pockets,
We look to our own lead filled faces,

Under the rain we fall together; in the nothing, begun nothing, before nothing.
The horses eat slate under the skies, over the earth.
but plough the darkened furrows under stones with hands like thunder.
The undulating landscape and its sheep grazed hills do not unwind

Plate xxi Lisa O'Brien, fieldwork in upper Glen Nevis with Peter Lanceley, August 2014
Source: London Fieldworks

Plate xxii   Mark Vernon field-recording at the Loch Eilde Mor hydroelectric generating station, Kinlochleven, July 2014
Source: London Fieldworks

Plate xxiii   Mark Vernon, *vox pop* at Cameron Square, Fort William, July 2014
Source: London Fieldworks

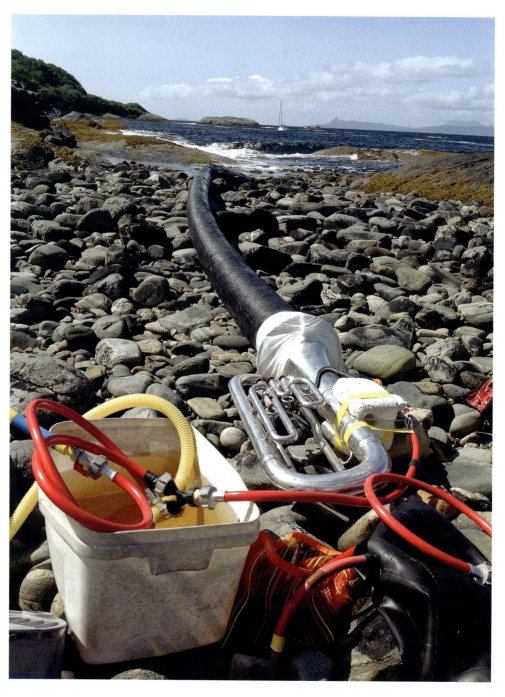

Plate xxiv *Big Pipe*, Loch Ailort, August 2014
Source: Courtesy of the artist Sarah Kenchington.

Plate xxv Sarah Kenchington, *Euphonium at Sea*, Loch Ailort, August 2014
Source: London Fieldworks

Plate xxvi *Generic Highland Hybrid Host 1*, installation at *Outlandia*, 2013
Source: Courtesy of the artist Clair Chinnery

Plate xxvii Aftermath of Clair Chinnery, *Generic Highland Hybrid Host 2*, August 2014
Source: London Fieldworks

Plate xxviii *The Boatswain's Call*, video still, Glenuig, August 2014
Source: Courtesy of the artist Clair Chinnery

Plate xxix Bram Thomas Arnold, *Swearing An Oath To A Scottish Glen*, performance still, *Remote Performances*, Glen Nevis, Scotland, August 2014
Source: London Fieldworks

Plate xxx *A Message to the International Hacker Community*, August 2014
Source: Courtesy of the artist Goodiepal and London Fieldworks

Plate xxxi Goodiepal posting *A Message to the International Hacker Community*, August 2014
Source: Courtesy of the artist and London Fieldworks

Plate xxxii Lee Patterson, field recording, upper Glen Nevis, August 2014
Source: London Fieldworks

Plate xxxiii Lee Patterson and Bruce Gilchrist, field recording, Loch Ailort, August 2014
Source: Inga Tillere

Plate xxxiv   Ruth Barker, *Remote Performances* broadcast, 7 August 2014
Source: Inga Tillere

Plate xxxv Ken Cockburn and Alec Finlay, *Remote Performances* broadcast, 8 August 2014
Source: Inga Tillere

Plate xxxvi   Resonance Radio Orchestra, *Remote Performances* broadcast, 9 August 2014
Source: Inga Tillere

SLATE

Picturing: A mind making the sound of this spade, and eyes the colour of the stone.
The surface is a clay-based aggregate, or perhaps slag from the separation of metal and ore.
The sound of a spade slicing the topsoil and hitting buried stone two inches down.

IGNEOUS

In the hollow of my front door step I might set a stone, for baking. I will stretch my budding roof across the rag of stars. Straining and extending I will root like wild garlic, laying the brick shock of my foundations, feeling the fragrance of my empty cellars taking shape as my walls break the surface. In the springtime I will germinate.

METAMORPHIC

Flower, I miss you.
If you sang me it would be the sound of a spade.
If you were to build me I would be sackcloth and peat stacked on a grate, with my perfume as the scent of the burning.
You may see me in a white dress stained by digging, with a mouth the colour of earthworms.
Grasses matted. I weave, and the clod comes down like something.
Here I am, Here I am (I am, I am, I am).
I need no-one. I am old as Grandmother Spider and as long as the sibylline shadow at my feet. I lick away the sediment with a viscous tongue of story. Limey morsels dry between my lips, choke my teeth and palette, and I swallow them in clotted lumps. The eating of clays is a lifetime of seeing; a consummation of time and the geoid span. I thumb down the sod with my toes.
I am Echo, prophetess of cosmic geomancy.

METAMORPHIC

And I will laugh, at the cinders in my hair. And the trees will burn to cinders on my skin, and the air will flame to nothing in my nose, and the night will be incinerated, bleached white and dead by hot compression of my hands. When I am igneous I will heave and split apart the world, vent forth and tear and burn in red and yellow horror splitting the coast and raining fire upon the surf. I will turn up. I will turn down. I will stay in. I will take up. I will move along. I will take down. I will bring back. I will shut up. I will stop out. I will move up. I will move through. I will turn out. I will wrap up.

WHEN I AM IGNEOUS

I sigh.
Down deep, all fire and liquid heat. Below it is the hot and molten core of me. My belly-button, sunk in flesh. They are my sloughed skin. These elements are my mnemonic, holding traces of my memory intact, as bound descriptors.

carbon C
sulphur S
manganese Mn
phosphorus P
hydrogen H
titanium Ti
magnesium Mg
potassium K
sodium Na
calcium Ca
iron Fe
aluminium Al
silicon Si
oxygen O

It peels off: Beneath it, my flesh is new, pink and raw, untried and vulnerable still. It itches, like a scab. The belly crust is thin, and on it rests the world. About my shoulders are two colures, great imaginary disks that intersect at the poles and dip in an inordinate ellipse toward the crust of my naval. Above the reach of my head, spangled through the split ends of my hair, is the geocorona. The earth is layered in a systematic mass.

My granite face is dusky in the firelight, and I hang from all the days and times of marble. I snake into the limbs and lungs of chasms, form them, push them out as pin-heads in the table top plateau.
I push against the marks already made, colubrine inveterate as The First Dilemma. I hear the sound of breathing to the crust's hushed grate; lush crushed prime in the darkness.

MY HANDS ARE SEDIMENTARY

Clack clack, clack clack, and catch it. I am Echo, grown old, still lonely, only a voice in the wilderness, calling and calling until I go away, lost in the hollow of a throat. Sticks and stones do make my bones and words come tumbling after. I am a goddess, old, with wrinkled tights and housecoat. They're thick as rocks, long as faultlines. I read the lines on my own hands. I feel as old as stone. My knees creak. An old old woman with dirt between her teeth, swinging her legs. Here I am at last.

I throw my tongue's clack clack, and catch it in my ear. You cannot see me. I am bigger than you. Stick your spade into my clay. Cut my turf. Dig anywhere in me. Dig anywhere.

I have mud and blood and clay and spit. What do you have in your mouth? Bees and stamens, pollen grains and breezes. Dig softly. That's it. Yes. I see the detritus of centuries. I see hundreds of years of things lost and thrown away and broken and soiled. I see who we were, but might not have been, and could have been again. I see things from the past. Dig deeper. Dig deeper. I see that something has been burnt here. I see the soil a different colour. I see a shape in the mud where wood has rotted away. What do you see? Something made of bone. Something made of dark metal. Coins. Amphora. What do you see? Take it grain by grain. Be gentle. Scrape away my topsoil with brushes. Dig down into me. In my belly I hold the past.

Do you wish to know me, now after all these years? I dwarf you. I am acres beneath your feet, and my mountains tower vast over your horizon. I am limestone and mud, magma and tectonics. So, I am a dark continent.

I am the deciduous woodland and the rainforest and the plantation and the scorched earth and the dump. I am the cornfield and the desert and the machair and the moorland heathers. I am the stone that runs under mountains and the mud that hold rivers to their beds. I am a contested borderland. I am the mapping of territories and the eating of soil. I am the soil that roots beneath walls, between picket lines, and barbed wire fences. I am geography and I am geomancy.

I am geography. I am mighty geography. I am strata. The sky arcs over me. The oceans lap at my circumference. My tornado. My mudslide. My avalanche. My earthquakes roar. My volcanoes erupt. My springs well up and spill fresh water. So, my forests dig their roots into my soil. So, the breeze runs over my topography. So, I am a dark continent.
So, I am a dark continent.

Sewn in stems, and waiting. At base. And here am I.
Thick bolts; of silence, shorn and mastered.
On the every day of sacred texts, and eating;
On speech unfolding time, and limping licking tongues;
Lent lyric structure to experience;
On the sets of terms for restoration disillusion,
On the outside typewritten insecticidal rainways;
Down stairs like open throats.
Woven,
On the cartograph eviscerate, all like lace and slipping,
On longing, with its mouse-feet fingernails;
On the tree grown limbs of the halo spaces;
On the belly-sound in the odyssey's needle;

126   REMOTE PERFORMANCES IN NATURE AND ARCHITECTURE

On the lamplit faces, fag-end lighters;
Plied trade, and aching welts;
On curlews' wooden wings are paired,
On clay;
On porcelain;
On the green-cut grass and whining;
On plant life walled in plastic;
And of the opening on to, and up:
On structure. On structure. On the opening of lips,
The beginning. Here am I, thinking. I will collect my thoughts like pansies in the grass.

Echo. Echo. My voice is hoarse, and distant. But I am losing my hold. Utterance is imprinted here, once was, will be. Your lips trumpet in a crenulated O. In the night you may find my murmurs in badgers sets, my sighs under the talons of owls. Your pollen blows across the sound of me. In the soil you may find me whispering, in mushrooms. You are a splash of colour in springtime, brief and overlooked. I am a voice spread low over the hills. You are growing wild among the wild garlic. I am lost in the wind. You are a fading bloom by a forgotten waterway. I am Echo.

It has taken a long time. My throat is my own and the glottal stops flop without cease, without care, without story. I have cut myself loose. I am full of your words, too many. More. No more. And no more. I have spent an immortal lifetime swallowing your words, and spitting them back. The words that make me who I am build me in their mass and weight. Here. I am as wide as skies. And as I leave I look over my shoulder, resting my chin on the mountain. Where did they go? My hands are translucent, and fading. I am a scuff mark, your footprint on wet shingle; who spoke this way before? I am un-remembered, as are you. I am a dream of something. Yours, perhaps. The mist is full of absent throats. The glen is full of whispered words, spoken elsewhere and thrown back. I let you. You flower, briefly, by my pools. I am become this place. My veins are thick with ringing minerals. I am heavy, grown stiff and calcified.

I am wedded, at last. And the water grows fat from my milk. I cup my lips to the shale and drink. I am suckled by the cracks between the hills. I suckle the land that I am. Breasts and moss. Wrists and heather. Hair and damp earth. Skin and soil. Thighs and peat. My throat is pressed against bark, under rain-laden thighs. My fingers grow into the soil. The land opens itself to my body. My body opens itself to the land.

I am Echo.
I am Echo.
I am Echo.
I am Echo.
I am Echo.
I am Echo.
I am Echo.
I am Echo.
I am Echo.

I am old as stone. You are brief. We hardly ever touch. Every year I see you bloom and die. Under the ground you lie, bulbous and dormant, poking your yellow head above the soil in spring and nodding nodding, only to crumple, fade, and turn to mulch. You are my pale and perishable lover. Above the earth below the sky, caught in the pines like a bag on a bough, rustling. I am an Echo.

Genius Loci. Echo.

Into *Outlandia*

Johny Brown

Fig. 43   Johny Brown MCing *Remote Performances*, August 2014
Source: Inga Tillere

THE MODERN TALE 1

We had travelled up from London, thinking the change of air would do us good. To tell the truth we were after finding a zeitgeist song for our band and the Scottish Folk Ballad at that moment was both zeit and geist: very beard.

It was kind of my idea: I initiated the trip up here. To be honest I had to do something to keep forward momentum. We all knew this was our last chance as a unit to stay together, to stay close, for the circle to remain unbroken.

We had to find a song that would make us whole again, and the city wasn't providing. So the management bods paid our fares up to Scotland and told us, by all means, to re bond re boot and find a folk song we could hype.

Being in a band is a funny thing and quite hard to keep together. There were four of us and we had been playing music since boarding together at performance school. I often felt like we were brothers, but sometimes not.

When a band works it is the best thing in the world. Musically, of course, and dare I say, on some great spiritual level. It had started us on the road to women cars wine and mortgages anyway, and it was a very comfortable attractive and fulfilling lifestyle all told.

Then the public stopped buying CDs and that queered the pitch somewhat. In theory it should not have bothered us because we had such a healthy digital presence, but then consumers discovered the free download.

Hmmm, things changed slightly for us then and I think our art suffered a little bit as a result, but hey, we were dedicated musicians devoted to our craft and furthermore bills needed to be paid, families cared for, habits maintained, all that jazz, we did not want to stop, we needed a new direction fast.

The other three were the jokers of the band and being used to London's charms they were very hard to impress. The journey up had been one of incessant gripes and few jokes. I was pensive when we arrived at Fort William.

But in the *Ben Nevis Inn* last night they looked as if they were beginning to enjoy themselves and joke a bit again. Especially when they got talking to this ancient arcane looking folk musician at the bar. He was authenticity itself.

We began plying him with whisky in exchange for tales, of which he had more than plenty, and which he dispensed in the coarse smiley local vernacular. But when Julian asked him if he had a song he could sell us his face darkened.

'Song, what do you mean …'

'Song, old man, particularly the song you have just sung …'

The ditty he had just sung very much appealed. It seemed to possess elements of drinking, sex, magic and horror within its versified walls and lacked any kind of sop romantic content whatsoever. The lyric alluded to a cold blow of wind … The song had possibilities.

'Got no songs lad, not for the likes of you.'

Ben said that we would pay him good money, nothing inherently life changing you understand, but, enough to buy a new vehicle, a Sky subscription, decent clothes or the latest model I-phone … at the very least.

We would no doubt change the lyric slightly, and transpose everything up a key. That was very much standard practice in these cases. Appropriation it was called in the trade, and I must say it is a craft in itself.

What we wouldn't do, we promised, would be to stick a grime or dubstep or God forbid a trance beat under the song, neither would we stick a cheesy rap on top. We would contemporise slightly though. Think digital ukelele and auto tune.

We would take an arrangement credit against any possible future profits and he would be more than happy with the lump sum we were about to offer. Weirdly, he snarled. Ben tried to place the offer into a more reasonable context.

'I mean come on old man, decent renumeration for what is a pretty isolated therefore quite presently worthless song.' Dan and Julian nodded. It was something any fool could see.

The man, very simply, growled. 'This song is priceless it can't be bought.'

'Everything can be bought, these days, and we wouldn't dream of stealing it, but being inspired by your song might be something else again.'

'This song is not just priceless, it's a danger, if played in the hands of fools, young fools such as yourselves'.

'That's why we'd like to hear you sing it especially for us.'

'Oh aye?'

'Yes, nobody could ever sing the song like you.'

'Why do I get the feeling you four blithe young idiots are taking a rise out of me?'

'We honestly love the way you sang it, when can we hear it again, we must hear it again?'

'I'll be singing it up at *Outlandia* tomorrow night.'

'*Outlandia*?'

'Aye, it's a place up on the mountain overlooking Nevis. People use it for various things. I often go up there to sing and what have you. I'm very much into *Outlandia* if you like. Treacherous up there though … And not to everyone's taste, but if you can find us, aye, you'll hear my song alright, and I tell you this for nowt, it will change yon lives forever'.

'Great,' I replied 'that's exactly what we are after, a song that will change our lives forever. We will rendezvous with you up there tomorrow.'

'Listen you young scamps, up there, things can happen and no one will ever know!'

'Things? What things?'

'Things is all I'm saying, I know what you're after and you'll get it alright, aye, every last bit of it.'

He then disappeared into the night leaving the barmaid to tell us more local tales as we plied ourselves with the local ales and whiskies. She could really talk and I vaguely remember bits of one of her tales, the four hunters and four vixens, after asking after, 'Four of your strongest spirits love.'

THE ANCIENT TALE

'Four of our strongest spirits coming up …

Now … the tale of the Four Hunters and the Four Vixens … some hundred years ago four hunters went hunting to the braes of Lochaber. Which is just up behind here. After the day's sport was over, they got to a summer-pasture bothy to pass the night.

They reached the bothy in the dark and set about kindling a fire. It had been a chill damp miserable day and all four hunters were soaked cold to the bone and in need of warmth and cooked provisions. A good fire soon roared.

After a supper, they sat about the hearth and began to talk. They loosened up a bit, and three of them said in fun that they wanted nothing now but to have their sweethearts with them there to make them as happy as kings.

"Goodness between me and that wish," said the fourth hunter.

The conversation then ceased, and the three hunters withdrew to a corner of the bothy, but the fourth stayed where he was. Shortly after that, four women entered the bothy.

They looked and behaved like the sweethearts of the hunters. Three of them went over and sat beside the three hunters in the corner; but the fourth stood before the hunter who was seated at the fire.

When the hunter sitting at the fire noticed this, he drew his dirk from the scabbard, and laid it across his knees. Then he took two trumps out of his pocket, and began to play on them. The woman noticed this and said:

> *"Good is the music of the trump,*
>
> *Saving the one note in its train.*
>
> *Its owner likes it in his mouth*
>
> *In preference to any maid."*

The hunter pretended not to hear her, but went on playing on the trumps as before. Then she began to come nearer, and tried to lay hold of him with her hand, but he kept her off as well as he could with his dirk.

When she failed in getting hold of him in this way, she tried another. "Give me a pinch of snuff," said she. The hunter prepared the snuff and reached it to her on the point of his dirk.

When she saw this, she turned the point of her elbow towards him and said, "Put it here." The hunter suspected that she would try to get a chance to seize the hand that held the dirk, and so he was on his guard.

As soon as he noticed she was about to stretch out her arm while he was reaching her the snuff, he kept the point of his dirk towards her, and gave her one or two prods with it.

That was enough. She went back to the other side of the fire, and stood there, irritating him. At length he heard the crowing of a cock as if on a hilltop.

"Over there," said the woman on the other side of the fire … "Is the black cock of March, it is time to depart." She said no more, but made for the door, and her three companions sprang out after her. As soon as daylight appeared, the fourth hunter went over to the corner.

And there he found his three comrades cold and dead with their throats cut and every drop of blood sucked out of their veins. Now he had no doubt that the women were vixens.

And the fourth would have done the same thing to him had it not been for the words and other means he had used.'

THE MODERN TALE 2

'And the fourth would have done the same thing to him had it not been for the words and other means he had used.'

I was still pondering on the words the barmaid spoke last night as we made our way out of the car park and up onto the brae. We were headed up and into a place called *Outlandia* and I was very hung-over.

The other members of the band looked considerably worse. Still, chin up, and all that. We paused a moment in the Braveheart car park and I could feel the weight of heritage pressing all around. The other three, not so.

We had awoken early at noon and then enjoyed a queasy pub lunch in the way of breakfast and reacquainted ourselves with a pint or two of the local Belhaven ale.

I had prepared a map that would take us up to the brae but Julian figured we wouldn't need it, as the app on his phone was much more precise, and would lead us straight to wherever it was we wanted to be.

He was a bit tetchy this morning and can sometimes start acting quite superior, which he is not very good at, but turns into a real pain for everyone else, so to humour him I threw the map. Besides I had the same app on my phone.

I missed the map though. The map was a tangible thing and looked good, artisan, folk almost. The song we were after was proving to be less tangible. All we had to go on was a melody and some scattered bits of lyric.

Ben tried to recall the man's words, but came out with. *'Four southern blades, from the garden they strayed, they soon found themselves on alien terrain, turn back where you came …'.* It was nowhere near the man's song at all.

Dan though picked up a melody and finished the first verse for him with a slight sarcastic air … *'Turn back where you came, with your fine English names, screams the wind and the mist, the cold and the rain.'* Hmmmmm.

We looked at each other; reluctant, boyish grins all round. The chemistry was back: we were a group again, doing the group thing. I loved this process where we threw all our ideas into the ring and sparked off each other.

Julian had brought a modest Takemine acoustic guitar fitted with light gauge metal strings and this had just the right timbre for the clean modern folk sound we were after. We sat down excitedly as he tuned the thing and off we went.

The sun blazed down as we ran over the initial lines and Julian strove to put a guitar line underneath, his fingers a blur of E minors and D majors and venturing up the fret to a brave B. We soon had something almost tangible.

Off we marched again up the brae as a collective chorus emerged, pertaining to our own knowledge of distant tradition. *'And the oak, and the ash, and the bonny ivy tree, that flourishes so softly in our home country'.*

I pulled my phone out to ring our management and tell them of this momentous breakthrough, no signal, damn I would have to complain to my service provider again when I returned. Still, no time for such thoughts now.

Pylons stretched away in the distance, the only sign of modern civilisation at all. Otherwise we were totally liberated from present culture. It felt quite enervating.

Dan was riffing on a second verse. *'But in Lochaber's braes, they go hunting all day, no song having bagged, they find a bothy to stay, and there in the dark, they build themselves a fire, and drink in the flame and talk of past bawdy times.'*

Superb, we all piled straight in on the chorus. *'And the oak, and the ash, and the bonny ivy tree, that flourishes so softly in our home country.'* Did you see what we did there, or rather, what we are achieving here …

Quite a clever conceit of self-reference, we have assimilated the tale told to us by the barmaid last night, and have ourselves assumed the role of the four hunters, only we are aiming to bag a song.

Of course the four hunters fail to bag their prey but we are already well on the way to bagging a song, being the smart young types that we are. The old man will be rueing the day he turned down our grand offer for his paltry song.

We had started out late in the afternoon and what a pleasure now to see a fine sun setting into the glen, we really were a roaming in the gloaming with twilight a gleaming and the four of us dreaming, the evening heather quite ablaze.

And then the midges descended and started going all dreek on us. We had come prepared though and I had brought some Autan Tropical repellent which was smooth and dry on the skin.

I gave first offer of this to Dan and he liberally coated himself before denigrating Ben's cheaper Boots version. Ben was most affronted and I laughed heartily as they began an aerosol joust.

Dan won easily having unloaded the entire contents of the can in Ben's face. I picked up the empty can and realised I had no protection against the flying irritants now. I appealed to Julian for a blast of his but he turned away from me.

The midges came down in droves. The higher we climbed the more they attacked me. The other three walked on unscathed. I started scratching and the other three started laughing at me.

I scratched and I scratched and I scratched and I scratched. Oh God how I scratched. Oh God how it hurt. Oh God how I wanted it to stop. The scratching just went on, bite upon bite upon bite, scratch upon scratch.

I wanted Julian to know just how much I was beginning to suffer and held out my arms. 'Look how swollen they are.'

'Well, not as swollen as your head generally is,' he replied.

Julian would pay for that remark later I hoped.

Sudden shift in the climate. A sweep of cloud came in from nowhere and rain as cold as sleet descended. There in front of us a half-hearted rainbow appeared. I was drawing blood with my scratching now. I couldn't stop.

A stone lodged itself in my boot but what the hell, I took the footwear off and marched barefoot up the rugged path, feeling the crunch of nature under my feet. I stepped on a slow worm thing which slithered off.

Dan and Ben insisted though that it was a snake, in actual fact, an adder, and I had probably been bitten. They were taking great delight in my discomfort as they described all the different ways a snake bite could kill.

I ventured on undaunted. In fact I felt quietly heroic. Like we were Wordsworth and Coleridge and a couple of other poets transported to the Highlands. Boswell and Johnson say, indomitable anthropological spirits on a Mission for song. I was feeling quite alone, detached from the group and strove to get back into step.

Louche clouds appeared overhead and looked quite dramatic so we stopped for a band photo. Delivery Fail! Quite frustrating that I couldn't communicate our present location and new image to our fan base via Instagram.

Outlandia was a modern bothy built in the forest. The old man might well be there and we could regale him with our new song that we wrote together. The old folkie would be sick with jealousy.

I decided to go off path for a while and strode through the fern and the bracken and jumping the streams, fair dancing around the sheep, as I sang our new song. I rejoined the path. My feet hurt. The band smiled to see me again.

We soon had the third verse nailed and talked of the four sweethearts from one of the tales we had been told last night. 'Bring those four minxy vixens on', exclaimed Julian in puckish delight, 'it will be love on a mountain top tonight.'

Something started bugging me when Julian said that. Like a shadow passed over me. That was such a non-folk thing to say! Was I becoming slightly too analytical of the whole trip. Love on a Mountain Top? Hmmmm.

I was feeling a kind of burrowing in my leg so I stopped at a path side bench and inspected my skin. Tiny black specks could be seen. Tics! Evil little bugs of the worst kind. We had come prepared though.

Julian wielded the special Tic tweezers. He told us there was a special technique to the job, that you had to circle the tweezers clockwise to pull the little bastards out. I was sure it was anti-clockwise. But Julian insisted he was right.

He was wrong! And already I could feel the detached bodies of the tics burrowing into my skin, alien parasite beings intent on sucking the very life blood out of me. I was starting to become very dizzy.

Sudden shift of scenery! A sign to *Outlandia* presented itself and we turned off the footpath and onto a wooden trail that led through the forest. I experienced a moment of true beauty as we walked amongst these trees.

Everything around us was coated in differing shades of green moss and the sun shone through the trees and the rain dripped down off the branches. I felt quite calm with a wonderful sense of peace within me.

The boardwalk traversed a steep gorge all of a sudden and deep below a burn gurgled. Ben and Dan were dawdling way behind and Julian stood gazing over the side in awe. I took advantage of the moment and laying a fraternal hand on his back I pushed.

It was quite thrilling and a little scary to see my erstwhile band member plummet through the air below me. He must have been pretty shocked himself for nary a scream passed his lips. Bar one unearthly shriek.

I carried on my way. I didn't have a clue what I would say to the other two. I would just have to make something up. I scratched some more. I was quite enjoying the scratching now. Blood dripped down on the boardwalk. I felt like I was part of the landscape at last.

And there it was up ahead, just like in the tale, *Outlandia*, our bothy. 'What exactly is a bothy anyway?' Dan had asked. 'Bothy,' I had replied patiently: 'A basic shelter: usually left unlocked and left for anyone to use free of charge.'

Scarlett Johansson had suffered grief inside a bothy, in a cool film that she was involved in recently. 'They are remote places,' I had informed Dan, and gave a brief description of the structure where Johansson suffered her unfortunate incident.

'Well, I hope it has wi-fi,' he had said.

'It will not' I replied. *Outlandia* was bereft of signal too. But it was warm and dry and just as well because a shift towards inclement conditions had occurred. I pulled the butane out of my pack and set it to flame.

How do I describe *Outlandia*? An amazing structure of wood hanging nest-like over the forest and looking straight on to Ben Nevis. I right off knew it to be a special place, where things might happen.

My legs though were aching and every bit of my body seemed to have swollen, but I felt great presence of mind as I made Ben and Dan a special cup of tea for when they arrived.

They drank the cup of tea I had made them and then began a civilisation bitch, 'but my phone signals vanished, my phone batteries are dead.' That kind of moaning. After a while they asked where Julian was?

I gave a surprised look. 'Oh, I thought he was with you!' I bade them go find him and reluctantly they agreed. They walked out drowsy from the tea into the thick mist and rain that had descended. The wind began to howl.

Somehow I thought they would not be returning. My supposition was rewarded when I heard them slip off the boardwalk and plunge down to the burn. It was just myself and *Outlandia* now.

Soon I had a fire raging too, which was just as well because heavy, heavy rain was descending and the evening had grown more than chill. I felt warm enough in my Scandinavian fisherman's jersey and Folk cagoule, but still …

Waves of fever-like delirium started to surge through me and I drank a cup of the special tea that I had prepared for Ben and Dan. It made me very drowsy and quite dreamy and my mind began to wander somewhat.

Rummaging around the hut I discovered an old tape machine, a portable Uher of the type used by sound boffins back in the dark ages of the Seventies, think Delia Derbyshire and BBC radiophonic workshop, that earnest lab-coated scene.

Let me describe this archaic device. It was a heavy squat box thing, in metallic grey. It was called the Uher 4000 Report Monitor and had really beautiful sound meters, and things to make the tape speed up and slow down.

It used an ancient form of reel to reel tape and had silver metal, pause, record, play, rewind and fast forward counters on it. What more can I say? What more do I want to say? A machine's a machine for all that.

Where on earth did this thing come from though? From avidly reading my *Wire* I deducted it probably belonged to Lee Patterson or Geoff Sample who would have been up here doing a field recording and had left it behind.

I was eager to hear what sounds they had been recording. Probably Eagles, Albatrosses, sorry, Gannets, and other Gaelic birds of impressive soaring wingspan and harsh guttural cry! I turned the power on. Its batteries had held.

I pressed play and sat back and waited for Lee's fieldwork to entertain me. Damn! The wheezing sound of that arcane chancer from the Ben Nevis Inn last night filled the pleasant atmosphere of my bothy.

Good God, just listen to this …

A devilish growl and here was the song he talked about: Sample or Patterson had obviously captured the man in the field and probably perished as a result, and now I was listening to the dread deathly words as they echoed off the wooden walls of *Outlandia*.

> *'You men betray your one true love, and in the grave you'll lay tonight*
>
> *You men betray your one true love, and in the grave you'll lay tonight*
>
> *Cold blows the wind, cold are the drops of rain.'*

Well it was down to one man now and cold indeed was the wind as the bothy door suddenly burst open and not four, but just one, sweetheart entered into my hut and quite simply gleamed in front of the fire.

By God, she was beautiful. I immediately recognised her, not as any vixen, but as the sexy alien character from the film *Under The Skin* which I had already watched five times this year and was quite fixated on, though the book is undoubtedly better.

The mission of the character she plays is to drive around Scotland sucking the life-force out of unsuspecting males via the medium of sex abetted by a really undeniably pucker, cut glass, English accent.

The males seemed to be dissolved into some kind of mercurial ether which was then packaged as some form of battery material. And here she was now. She had come for me. I could see a troubled night ahead.

Having seen the film so many times, I knew that, obviously, she was an alien, but her breasts were just, so, bloody becoming, and now they were becoming onto me and *Outlandia* was getting that liquid etherworld feel.

The Dark Haired Alien Johansson moved closer. I scratched a further itch and quivered inside. I wanted to be brave and strong and assertive, but all I could do was stare, and scratch … I bit my lip hard.

She had applied red lipstick and the fur coat she wore played on all my senses, exploiting certain weaknesses and prejudices I held. She was going to suck the life out of me. I thought of the Barmaid's words the previous night … 'And the fourth would have done the same thing to him had it not been for the words and other means he had used.' I saw clear as night what I was expected to do. But hell, I had no trumpet, no dirk, not even a pinch of snuff to utilise. Besides, I wanted to succumb. Badly.

'Stand back,' I said, remonstrating with my free hand whilst my other hand scratched my bites and suppurations. The tics had burrowed right into the midge bites now and I was having no respite from their parasite dance. My perception started to splinter somewhat.

She became the barmaid last night became the old man of arcane song became my mother my sister became the oak and the ash and the bonnie ivy tree became my lost band mates became everything I loved and despised desired and feared in one dread vision.

She came closer and I thought this is the moment. My just desserts for what I did to my blessed band mates, for having want away thoughts from my blessed partner, for wanting to appropriate and pervert the blessed folk song!

This is it! She will eat me alive, consume me whole, oh terrible end, and not a thing I can do about it. I stood up and discarded my clothing and opened my arms and beckoned her to take me, and in the moment of rural horror, time itself seemed to stand still.

I moved towards the fire as she did. At least she would get a good look at this fine specimen of urban indie type band musician she was about to devour. I closed my eyes and waited and waited and waited.

Finally I could wait no longer and opened my eyes again. She was up close and staring at me in fascinated horror. I smiled and she recoiled and an unearthly shriek rent the forest. She turned and fled.

Wow, I had never suffered rejection before. I pulled a mirror out of my rucksack and gazed in shock at what I saw. I was a living writhing mess of scratch and bite and blood and scab and bile and pus. I was filth itself.

And then the real visions kicked in and I was assailed by wild thoughts, weird propositions, strange prophecy, all undercut by unsure memory and distrust of the present, until I no longer knew who I was, where I had been or where I was going.

I wished I was back in Dalston! I wished I was back on those firm Hackney streets walking under comforting sodium lights, with all manner of people surrounding me. A night of film at the Rio, a bite to eat at Red, up to the Rochester for a drink with the band after rehearsals at Gunfactory Studios or Audio Underground, alas,

The dreams I experienced were like none I had experienced before. Many visions and situations presented themselves before me. I was overwhelmed with possibilities. At some point I must have crashed out.

Then after many hours of oblivion the Uher kicked into sudden life, a field recording of Hooded Crows and Golden Eagles. Storm Petrels and rutting Stags bellowed forth, and like a signal I jolted back into real life.

I couldn't believe the ordeal I had just undergone. The fire had burned down to just the embers now and even they were turning to ash. Dawn brought a stark realisation. My three band members lay out there in the wilderness.

There was no doubting that they were dead, deep in a glen where no one would ever find them, left to decompose, for the wildlife to pick at their bones. I would have to make up a story when I returned.

The uncomfortable and piercing thought then struck me, *where to from here?* I would miss my fellow musicians dearly and would never get another band to replace them, how could I?

That in itself was not such a bad thing mind.

Not now that I had overcome the Alien Johansson and had possession of the folk song and what's more had just suffered a great many strange unruly visions that would serve my lyric writing for years to come.

In this trade the best artists are solo, think Alasdair Roberts, or his label mate Bonnie Prince Billy.

Not strictly Scottish true, with that particular singer songwriter emanating from Chicago, but he had the name, and the chops, and that's what counted. I had the chops and the song and I would just have to change my name. Something appropriately Gaelic maybe?

This whole night had been such a game changer I realised, and counted myself so lucky, charmed almost. The things I had learned in the course of the night, why, it was just like Robert Johnson coming back from the crossroads after selling his soul to the devil.

I had just undergone a very similar experience, and the new deal was, is, that I head back to the city armed with songs that would both change the world for the good and make me undeniably and filthy rich.

The responsibility was mine now. It felt like a heavy weight, but an exhilarating one. I am the Monarch of the Glen. I am the new king of folk. I am the bearer of terrible secrets. I it is who is timeless, arcane. An agent of change; I will carry the burden for you all.

I stepped out of the bothy and into the mist that had materialised. A fall of sleet descended and my bones were cold but my soul felt strangely afired. 'Things can happen and no one will know'. How true the old man's words were.

There would be no turning back. I couldn't see my feet in front of me, but carried on regardless, hobbling on my injured foot, scratching my open wounds, feeling, as if I had won something quite unattainable.

But then, quite detached, isolated and so, lonely, so alien, so unutterably alone. I felt abject, quite lost, quite dreek if truth be told. Maybe the solo folk thing wouldn't work for me, maybe my partner would not want me when I returned.

God these clouds and this rain, the shifting veil of clouds and the clinging of the mist, it really got inside your head in a most darkening manner. A man could lose his mind up here.

I concentrated on the job in hand and started up a dark mantra as I walked: 'folk folk folk folk folk folk folk folk folk folk folk.' My management would be pleased, they'd been badgering me to go solo for ages. Damn this rain.

Fig. 44 Uher reel to reel tape machine used in Johny Brown's live radio play *Into Outlandia*, August 2014
Source: Inga Tillere

But then the weather shifted again and the clouds swiftly vanished. A strong sun appeared in a clear sky and I realised in this moment of clarity that I had made a terrible mistake. I had got this whole thing wrong. My management had got it wrong. The band had got it wrong. Oh foolish errand. Folk was not where it was at. Not at all.

Maybe last year it might have been. But this year surely it was Northern Soul that was in vogue, and ripe for appropriation, how could our management have misled us so badly, how could I have let my band members slip away so easily?

Damn! It was just me now. All alone on this earth. But with a new world waiting. Northern Soul? The sound of heartbreak and melancholy set to jazz chords over a straight four four beat … Hmmmm! I must depart for Wigan immediately.

High-Lands

Tony White

Fig. 45   Tony White, *Remote Performances* broadcast, 6 August 2014
Source: Inga Tillere

Sitting on a mossy stone with a drawing board across his lap, looking down at the loch through the sparse and twisted branches of what from the shape of the leaves even he could tell was an oak of some sort, although it looked nothing like the ones at home, Chris stopped drawing and put down his pencil; then watched it roll down the paper and park itself against a fold of denim. He had been drawing for hours now. His protest had happened. He had removed himself from the celebration, rejected it, but beyond that, what? If anything each pencil-stroke was taking the drawing further in the wrong direction. This was not what he had wanted at all. And now it was beginning to get dark.

'You're cutting off your nose to spite your face, son,' Mr. Clegg the deputy headmaster had said, more Sergeant Major than teacher, but Chris hadn't cared. He had turned and walked straight to the art room, where the cartridge paper they'd stretched earlier in readiness for the following morning's watercolour class would by now be dry. Chris grabbed a drawing board and kept walking, the door swinging shut behind him.

What Mr. Clegg at dinner the evening before had pompously called 'a commission' – his offer to pay Chris five pounds to paint a Queen's Silver Jubilee banner that could be hung up behind the stage – had not been much of a consolation. If anything, it had added insult to injury. If Chris wasn't going to be allowed to take part in the end of term concert, Cleggy could stuff his sodding banner, fiver or not.

'What's that bird doing?' Andy had said, interrupting.

They had all turned around to look. A small bird outside the window was fluttering at the glass.

'He's trying to get in, look!' said Geoff.

'A bullfinch,' said Mr. Clegg. 'No, he's eating the midgies that are attracted by the light.'

Looking down across the treetops to the moonlit waters beyond, Chris couldn't see the camp at all from where he now sat. There was hardly a break in the trees. No roof-tops, no sign that the cluster of Nissen huts and other buildings were there, but they were; hidden in the forest.

The whole place appealed to a part of Chris that he still hadn't quite grown out of: boyhood games, adventure playgrounds. It reminded him of the dilapidated and overgrown assault courses that ran along beside the railway lines between Guildford and Aldershot. To Chris and his mates, a few tyres and nautical-looking objects, floats of some kind, hanging from a damp tree, still suggested play, even if the old lunchtime games of 'best man dead' or 'Germans v the rest' were several years behind them.

When they had arrived a few days before, driving up the hill at the end of what had been a twenty-four hour coach journey from Surrey, Chris had felt just as excited as he always did at the start of a holiday, even if he was going to be spending the week with people that he'd be leaving behind in a week or two, and plenty more that he didn't care if he ever saw again. Among Chris's older school friends, Geoff had already got a job lined up in Woking, as a junior clerk for an insurance company. He would be starting in July and his parents had given him a new, black

Plate xxxvii   Band of Holy Joy, *Remote Performances* broadcast, 8 August 2014
Source: Inga Tillere

Plate xxxviii Stuart Brisley, *Untitled Landscape* (verso), 31 cm x 53.5 cm, watercolour on card, 2 June 1953. Photo: Andy Keate
Source: Courtesy of the artist.

Plate xxxii Stuart Brisley, *Untitled Landscape* (recto), 31 cm x 53.5 cm, watercolour on card, 2 June 1953. Photo: Andy Keate
Source: Courtesy of the artist

Plate xl   Props for Band of Holy Joy, *Into Outlandia*, 8 August 2014
Source: Inga Tillere

leather briefcase for Christmas, in anticipation. Andy was following his dad into the Post Office. One or two others in their class had got places at university. Chris's own family had had a bit of a talk about it, too, one Sunday, what Chris was going to do, when his grandparents had been over for tea. Chris's father had suggested a career in British Rail, but that was the last thing he wanted to do.

'But Christopher, you need something to fall back on.'

'Your father is right,' said his grandfather. 'Where's your LSD going to come from?'

'He means pounds, shillings and pence dear,' said his grandmother. Then, seeing the dismay on Chris's face, she had said, 'Oh, well. You're drawing all the time. Why don't you become a draughtsman?'

'I'm going to do foundation,' he'd said. 'At Farnham, like Tim.'

'Or an architect?' said his mum. 'If you've got a skill you should put it to good use. Learn a trade.'

The old army huts that made up the camp were still decorated with odd bits of militaria, which Chris supposed had probably just been left behind when the place was decommissioned. The refectory was decorated with aircraft and tank recognition silhouettes, semaphore flags, a twenty-four hour clock. There was a photograph of the Queen, too. In fact there was one in every room, except for the bogs.

'Soon sort that out,' Chris had said, imagining hanging one in every cubicle – or down every pan – but the picture frames were all securely screwed to the walls.

When he, Geoff and Andy had gone exploring in the woods, they'd found a dump containing the kinds of things that had not been screwed down: rusting filing cabinets, a Banda machine, refrigerators. Not the grenades and shells that Andy had been hoping for. There were no bullets or World War II helmets. Best of all were some thick, woollen jumpers in army green with shoulder and elbow patches, that were riddled with holes but not quite rotted. The most serviceable of them he had taken in to the bathroom, washed it through several changes of water, and now it was hanging up to dry on the verandah outside their room, where it still smelled like a wet dog, or worse. He would give it to his mum when he got home; to wash, not to repair. She could barely bring herself to say the word 'punk'.

Chris wished that he hadn't spent his last few 10p's calling home from the pay-phone in the refectory during breakfast, but he'd known that his parents were going to Hayling Island today, to see the Spithead Review, and that they were planning to stay for the illuminations, so he wouldn't be able to catch them again before the coach left tomorrow afternoon.

'Do you think we'll see the Queen?' she had asked.

'Of course not, mum,' he'd said, unable to resist the urge to rub it in. 'She'll be miles away. You'll be lucky to even see the Royal Yacht.'

'Well, your father is taking his binoculars,' she'd said.

'He'll need them.'

'Christopher?'

'What, mum?'

' … '

He could hear her blowing her nose at the other end, a sob: 'Mum?'

'Oh, Christopher! It's awful! Your father said not to tell you, that we should wait until you got back, but I said you'd want to know.'

Chris looked again at his drawing. It was pathetic. No wonder he nearly hadn't got in to foundation. He remembered opening the envelope that had arrived in the post a couple of weeks after he had gone for the interview. The rejection had made him feel numb. When he told Mrs Yearly in college later that same day, his A-level art teacher had turned almost white with rage. 'Right,' she'd said after a few moments. 'We'll see about that. I'm going over there right now.' Then she had simply turned and left the room.

Looking out of the window, Chris had seen her little orange Fiat 500 turning right out of the college car park a minute or so later. Whatever she had done once she'd got there, it had worked. He had received another – different – letter from the art school office the next morning. But looking at this drawing, maybe they had been right the first time. The idea that he could draw anything, let alone the near-infinitely complex leaf-scape before him seemed laughable. The stylised frieze of tree-like shapes that crossed the middle of the page in front of him had taken several hours to draw, but still looked scrappy and distant. He had wanted more than ever, today, now, to feel as if he were falling through the paper, to get lost in it – that feeling of inhabiting the world that he was drawing – but he couldn't get past the surface.

Gusts of laughter and music from the party were carried by the wind. Every now and then he could pick out a voice he recognised. Usually Chris loved the end of term concerts that happened whether they were on a trip or not. Everyone doing their party piece, whatever that might be. Ifor Thomas, Mr. Thomas, the pottery teacher, getting drunk and staggering up on stage to recite some Dylan Thomas in that great, booming, Welsh voice of his. You just said what you wanted to do, and you got up and did it – normally – then Cleggy would play 'The Last Post' on the bugle at the end. Well, Chris was sure he'd heard that half an hour or more ago, so the various acts, the concert itself, would certainly have finished by now, and even from this distance Chris could hear enough to know that he wasn't all that impressed with the local DJ's record collection. First 'Albatross', and now Rod Stewart, who was still talking about whatever it was that he didn't want to talk about. Geoff and Andy had been carefully planning for these slow numbers for weeks. Working out who they were going to dance with; hoping for a quick feel. Setting their sights too high, as usual. At this rate it would soon be time for the national anthem, again, for the umpteenth time. After this month, Chris didn't care if he never heard it again.

Even above the noise of the party, Chris could hear water rushing far below him in the glen. It was quieter now but the morning before when a day's worth of rain was finding its way down off the hills, the sound had been as bright and clear as a burst of static, and almost deafening. It reminded Chris of turning the telly up to full volume after the close-down, or listening to the big shortwave radio at Tim and Hugh's place. The twins were a year or so older than Chris. They also lived in the village, in one of the farm houses down behind the old hop kiln. Chris was one of the few who could tell them apart, and that was because Tim was his best mate. Tim had just finished foundation and was waiting to hear whether he had got in to art school in London. Chris would go over to Farnham and meet Tim at the college sometimes and go to the Queen's Head with him and his mates. 'Chris is really good', Tim would say. 'He's coming here next year, aren't you Chris?'

Tim's twin brother Hugh had started working with their father as a labourer on the farm. Mr. Harris had been stationed in Germany just after the war, doing his national service in a camp that must have been a bit like this one, but which had been very close to the border with East Germany, rather than up here in Scotland.

Sometimes, on nights when he wasn't working late, when they had come in from playing football, Mr. Harris would bring them cups of instant coffee and tell them stories about those days in the army. There'd be forty of us in this big tent, he'd say, lighting up a cigarette. Two long rows of receivers, and a glass office at the end for the brass. The best blokes sat at the end near the office, that was where the hardest work got done. All of us listening to numbers stations, transcribing, Morse code in those days, broadcasting from Russia, Poland and Hungary. Some of the broadcasts would last twenty-three hours and fifty-nine minutes, and somewhere in that there would be just one sequence of five numbers that was the code for whichever frequency the station would switch to for the next twenty-four hours, and you'd only have one minute to complete the calculations and retune.

He was a good storyteller, Mr. Harris, and when he said how tense it was, sitting there in silence for those few seconds, Chris could almost feel it. He imagined listening to the dead air, waiting for the station to come on again. Praying that he had identified the correct sequence. Most of the time they got it right, too, Mr. Harris said. Although some blokes went mad. Ripped off their headphones and fled screaming out in to the dark. Another one ran the length of the tent and threw himself through the glass into the office.

Mr. Harris told them that he had been put in charge of mops and buckets, and the burning of sensitive waste, which meant that when he wasn't sitting at the receiver with the bakelite headphones on his ears, he'd be counting duckboards and brooms, or piling reams of paper into the incinerators. It also meant that in the event of an invasion he would be one of the ones left behind. The cleaning detail, trying to destroy as much as they were able, before they were taken prisoner or worse.

'You boys don't know you're born,' he'd say. 'You're lucky.'

Then, Oh yes, some of it was a laugh, but it was a monumental waste of bloody time. Such an inefficient system. Kowtowing, but all the while just trying to get one over on whoever was giving the orders. You'd count the same ten rifles six times, just so you could say that there were still sixty of them like there were supposed to be.

It's a bloody good job there never was an invasion, Mr. Harris would say. If they counted the men the way we counted the rifles.

He said that one night they could hear the Russian tanks over the border, less than a mile away. A blizzard of numbers increasing in intensity to match the troop movements on the other side. We'd have to keep the engines of the trucks running all the time, he'd say; just in case.

Some evenings when they were around there, he and Hugh listening to records in Tim's room, they might also go out to one of the brick sheds out the back of the house, by the orchard, where Mr. Harris kept a big old shortwave radio. Once it had warmed up, they would take turns listening to the numbers stations. Mr. Harris had an old foolscap diary from 1960 in which, using several colours of pen and pencil, he had logged in tiny spidery handwriting the details of certain broadcasts over a decade or more. Some dates and times had been overwritten again and again, with additional flaps of paper sellotaped on top. Mr. Harris would flip it open to whatever day it was, and run his finger down the column to see when the next broadcast would be. 'Hungary,' he might say. 'You can tell by the phasing. Regular as clockwork, that one.'

Chris loved it. Listening to the sound of space, was what it felt like. A bottomless pit of sound, punctuated by the occasional bleep and chirrup, by snatches of music and foreign languages, noises that weren't even there. Numbers stations that would suddenly switch on if you knew where and when to look. Not Morse any more, but strangely-accented voices reading lists of numbers. Some broadcasts lasted just a few minutes, others went on for hour after hour. There was something hypnotic and musical about it that he enjoyed. This was why when Chris's mum and dad had offered to get him a transistor radio for Christmas he had checked with Mr. Harris first and then asked specifically for a particular little Grundig that was just the same as all the others, with its wood-effect plastic casing and telescopic aerial, but which could pick up shortwave, as well as medium wave for Radio 1. He had brought it with him on the school trip, too, together with a little earpiece that had been coiled up in the battery compartment when he had opened the box on Christmas morning. He'd brought it with him to camp, mainly so they could listen to the charts on Sunday night: 'Sheena is a Punk Rocker' down to number thirty-three, The Stranglers up to number sixteen with the double A-side of 'Peaches' and 'Go Buddy Go'.

'God Save the Queen' by the Sex Pistols, the song that Cleggy had forbidden Chris to perform at the concert – 'Over my dead body!' were his exact words – was down to number nine.

Chris wondered what the numbers stations would be doing right now, then what the forest might sound like if you could tune in to that teeming vastness. He wished that he had thought about it and brought the little Grundig up here, too.

He imagined that with the whole of the Royal Navy at anchor in the Solent, the aircraft carriers, the frigate squadrons and the flagships, the destroyers, the submarines, the minesweepers and the training boats, the survey ships and the hovercraft, the warships and the ships-other-than-warships, the Commissioners of Irish Lights, the Coast Guard, the Customs boats, the life-boats, the oil tankers, the cargo vessels, the tugs, the trainers, the public school boats, the training yachts, the ferries, the fishing boats, the foreign and commonwealth ships, the postal steamers and the auxiliaries, the miscellaneous units and the light vessels, the Royal Yacht Britannia: With all of that down there, what was left up here? And what was to stop an atom bomb wiping out the entire fleet? What if, right now, some armada of enemy vessels, unidentified and from who knew where – some other high land – was slowly breaking formation, fanning out to slip silently through the archipelago that was stretched out before him. Ships the size of islands dropping through the clouds to slice beneath the water without a ripple. Hostile vessels of unknown classification sliding past Hawe Bank and through Tiree, past Colonsay into the Firth of Lorne, past Scarba and Luing and Shuna. Obsidian craft gliding through the Lynn and into the Sound of Mull. The attack sequences of some vast power being blindly executed in concert from every loch, and every lynn and all across the moonlit sea. And this inverted fleet, this invasion, would be directed by its own codes; filling the airwaves, crowding the dial.

Chris imagined Mr. Harris listening in, right now, the only one able to understand what was going on. Yet even he would not be able to make sense of the horror; frantically turning the dial, but finding no answers there. No clear information, no five-figured sequence, no instructions, no space at all left in the airwaves, no interruption to the undecipherable cacophony that stretched into the darkness and the distance in every direction and at every point and as far as the ear could hear.

If it wasn't for this school trip, Chris had been supposed to go and see The Stranglers playing at The Roundhouse in Camden on Sunday, with Tim and a couple of his mates. They were doing two gigs, one in the afternoon and one in the evening. Tim had sent a postal order off weeks ago for two tickets for the four o'clock one.

'Don't worry, mush,' Tim had said, when Chris had told him that he couldn't go after all, because he had to come on the school trip to Scotland. 'I'll give Mark your ticket.'

Mark was one of Tim's friends who had also done the foundation course at Farnham. His family had a huge house in Haslemere.

'It's the kind of place where you need motorbikes to get to the bottom of the garden,' Tim had once said, and he wasn't joking.

Mark seemed nice enough most of the time, but once when they were at the pub when Chris had gone over to meet Tim after the Wednesday evening life-drawing class and when Tim was in the loo, Chris had heard Mark laughing about Tim and Hugh's house. 'Have you been there?' he was saying to Jenny, a girl who Tim liked to hang around with. 'It's so small. His father is a farm labourer. What do you think of Tim's work?' Then they had dissolved into giggles. Chris had been too embarrassed to challenge Mark, and then once Tim got back the conversation had picked up and he had forgotten about it, until now.

Tim had telephoned the camp to speak to Chris on the Sunday evening, when he got back from The Stranglers. When they'd answered the phone, Tim had pretended to be Chris's father, calling with an urgent message. Not having expected the call, Chris had been a bit worried to be summoned from the dinner table, but had pissed himself when he found out who it really was: 'Wotcher, mush!'

Of course, Tim had been calling to tell Chris about the gig. 'Do you know what "jubilee" means?' he'd asked.

Chris had said that he didn't.

'No, I didn't either, but it means "set people free",' Tim had said. 'But they're not, are they, with their gold coaches and their Spithead reviews; all that "send her victorious" crap.'

'My mum and dad are going to Hayling Island to watch it from there,' Chris had said.

'My dad will be listening-in to the boats on the radio, I expect,' Tim had said. 'Oh, but guess what.'

'What?' Chris had asked.

It turned out that when they were on the train back from Waterloo to Guildford after the Roundhouse gig, Mark had told Tim that he had got a place at the Royal College of Art. Tim had been pleased for his mate, of course, but by the time he spoke to Chris, the reality of it had sunk in and he was furious: 'Mark hasn't even done his degree! How could he go straight to the Royal College? His work's not that great. Bloody public school boy, that's what it is. He got a "special dispensation"! Can you believe it? If you're one of them, you can just walk in. The doors are opened for you.'

Chris put down the drawing board, then stood up and stretched his legs. Carrying the drawing under his arm, not caring if his sleeve rubbed the unfixed graphite, if the drawing got ruined, he began to pick his way back over the mossy rocks, the bracken and heather that led back to the path and through the denser woods. He walked past bramble and gorse, past glistening rocks that sprouted heather, oak and birch seedlings from the merest crack. The path was carpeted with needles and pinecones, but he did not really see it because he was miles away, still going over and over the conversation with his mother from the morning. He hadn't quite understood what she was saying at first. He had thought that she was talking about something here at the camp, the tyre swings. It just didn't make sense. Something about the tyres and floats hanging from the tree.

'What? The ones by the adventure playground?' he'd asked, puzzled.

'No,' she'd said, 'by the orchard gate'.

Which gate? Found what? What did she mean?

'No, it's not a buoy,' he'd said. 'They're not called buoys, they're floats. They use them for lobster pots. That's what Mr. Clegg said. I made that mistake as well.'

'What, my darling?' she had said. 'Can you hear me? No, I said here, in the village. One of the boys, the twins. Your father had to help poor Mr. Harris with the police and whatnot. There was a letter from St. Martins. Timothy didn't get a place. Well, you know he'd had his heart set on it, Christopher. It was Hugh that found him, when he went out on the tractor to feed the bullocks.'

As Chris got nearer to the camp, the path gave out on to the concrete-slabbed road. He jumped down the short drop and turned to walk towards the Nissen huts, which clustered around the larger of the yards. A rudimentary stage had been built up against one of the concrete, tank-inspection ramps. The DJ was set up on a table over by the refectory entrance. He was playing 'Lido Shuffle' by Boz Scaggs, and lining up another record. A couple of teachers were dancing. Chris wondered if there was any beer left, or if he might be able to cadge a cigarette and some whisky from anyone. By this time of night, Ifor Thomas was usually a good bet.

WRITING HIGH-LANDS

With a title that is an inversion of US author Thomas Pynchon's 1960 short story 'Low-Lands' – and noting particularly the Aloes Press 1978 UK edition of that story – my own short story for *Remote Performances* draws on the remote Highland setting of Lochaber in which it was written; imagining a former military base turned outward-bound centre as the site for a Sixth Form school trip.

'High-Lands' is also set within a number of other vectors of distance and remoteness that are continually measured or calibrated in the story: between the north and south of the British Isles, or east and west across the Cold War 'iron curtain'; between rural communities and arts education; between the drawing of a forest and the forest itself; between working class 'subjects' and a Queen who must be looked upon with binoculars in her Silver Jubilee year; as well as the temporal distance between 1977 and the present day, and the sudden irrevocable remoteness that is created by a friend's suicide.

The story also draws on then current research[1] with the British artist Stuart Brisley, including observations of his ten-day performance *Before the Mast*, at DOMOBAAL, London (21–30 November 2013), but focusing particularly on a number of conversations about his own experiences, first of attending Guildford School of Art in the 1950s and subsequently of national service – which turned into 'active service' – as a radio operator for the British Army at Langeleben on the then West German border with East Germany near Königslutter am Elm. The radio transmissions and frequencies that within the story are both monitored on behalf of the state and listened-to for fun (and which are echoed by the actual radio transmission of the story as a performance that was broadcast live from *Outlandia*) are both measured – charted! – and immeasurable.

With this story I had particularly wanted to try and turn up the volume, as it were, on a specific act of rebellion by the young Stuart Brisley, who pointedly spent Queen Elizabeth II's Coronation Day in June 1953 drawing the woods near his home (Plates xxxviii–xxxix), rather than joining in the celebrations with his family and the rest of the village. In order to amplify this small but significant act, I found that I needed to fictionalise and to transpose those few biographical fragments forward by a generation, to another Royal celebration that took place twenty-five years later – the Queen's Silver Jubilee – which introduced the additional momentum of punk, and the Sex Pistol's great republican anthem 'God Save the Queen'.

This fictionalising of Brisley's own accounts and the distribution here of fragmentary representations of his lived experiences amongst a fictional cast, the characters in the story, was also in part a test for a larger work of fiction exploring further consciously republican aspects of his later works, which at time of writing is ongoing. With 'High-Lands' then, I wanted to see how far (both literally and figuratively) from Brisley's spoken accounts I might need to take this material, and how I might utilise the various measures of time and remoteness enumerated above to create a fictional and reflected – yet critical – space for the reader, bearing in mind also a supposed dictum of the late US author Donald Barthelme that, you 'must break their hearts' (Appleyard, 2010, p. 10).

REFERENCES

Appleyard, Brian (2010) 'A Man Looking for Answers', *Culture* supplement, *Sunday Times*, 31 October, p. 10.

NOTES

1   A loose collaboration with Stuart Brisley, Maya Balcioglu and Dr Sanja Perovic of Kings College, London, that was made possible by Tony White's appointment as Creative Entrepreneur in Residence and Visiting Research Fellow in the French Department at Kings College, London, funded by CreativeWorks London.

Endnotes on Remoteness

Clair Chinnery

Lisa O'Brien

Bram Thomas Arnold

THOUGHTS ON REMOTENESS: 'ERE BE DRAGONS (OR CUCKOOS)
Clair Chinnery

Remoteness (geographic or psychological) is based on the idea of at least two relative positions. 'Here' and 'there', 'me' and 'you'. For 'a place', 'a terrain', 'a location' to be remote, it depends on where you are. If you are 'here', you are not remote. 'There', on the other hand, is another place entirely …

During *Remote Performances*, the Highlands were redolent with the idea that Scottish independence was a very real possibility. Although a British artist – born in 'England' – during my time in Lochaber, I found it easy to imagine why voters in the Scottish referendum would say 'Yes'. Its rich culture, politics and geography seemed so far removed from the metropolitan political powerbase of London with its proximity to my own home in Oxford. En route to Glen Nevis, I stopped to visit Housestead's Fort on Hadrian's Wall, and was reminded that the Roman name 'Britannia' referred *only* to the land to the South. Even the might of ancient Rome considered Caledonia to be very much 'another place', beyond the edges of 'that particular' empire. The timing of these experiences and locations, resonated, with my own practice, although it is the more recent Empires of Britain and Europe, their identifiers, impacts and legacies that have stimulated the development of many of my works.

Before the entirety of the earth's surface was accurately mapped, myths about the inhabitants of unknown lands and waters, beyond the edges of the 'known world' were widespread. Stories and rumours of strange beings and animals have found their way into the literature, art and oral histories of many cultures. Mermaids, Cyclops, Monopods and many more fantastical creatures have fuelled the imaginations of human ancestors, occasionally aided by travellers returning from unfamiliar landscapes, topographies and climates, populated by alien plants/ animals/humans and cultural signifiers.

How do we draw borders, and name places and things? This question is why I am so fascinated by birds. Their populations have no general respect for human ideas of 'naming and taming' geographies. The maps they make with their distribution, make un-recognisable countries from recognisable land masses and/or watery expanses. Such maps may be subject to the instability of seasonal 'shifting' when annual migrations take place. The wellbeing of their populations, however – like so many other non-human organisms – are contingent on the ecological effects of human activities. Geographical remoteness can promise two potential scenarios: one offering a sense of privacy or 'safety' made possible through sparse human population; another providing opportunities for simulations of manoeuvres (often by the military) planned for destructive applications elsewhere. This can disrupt our understanding of remoteness as a space for physical and psychological refuge. Remoteness in the imaginary, however, still has the potential to offer fertile possibilities for a range of creative approaches, possibilities and forms. For me, a well-hidden hut perched in a canopy of coniferous woodland in a remote Highland glen offers an irresistible testing ground.

NOTIONS OF CONTEMPORARY REMOTENESS
Lisa O'Brien

Driving home to the West from Inverness, in the black out of a moonless night, I turn off at Garve and don't see another car, or human and only a handful of mostly empty houses for the next hour. I don't have a mobile signal and the radio reception is nothing to write home about though I sometimes play the static at this point in the journey, just for a bit of company but the sudden, disembodied voices spluttering out a few random words can make me jump out of my skin. It's a fine line between comfort and terror. Search … search … search blinks on the radio's LCD screen.

On the same journey one night last month, driving down the single track road through Glen Torridon, past the giants of Liatach and Beinn Eighe, I come across a lorry at a 45 degree angle. It's tipping off the side of the road with its indicators flashing, an alarming tick in the blackness. I haven't seen anyone for miles, I can't phone anyone and realise, reluctantly, that I should probably find out if there is anyone in the cabin. The driver's side has lifted a few feet off the ground, so high I can barely see the steering wheel. I reach up and knock on the door, nothing. I try the handle, locked. Finally, and with great trepidation at the thought of what I might discover I climb up on the outside step of the cabin and peer over the door frame … nothing, no one, a profound emptiness.

I return to the car and squeeze by the lorry, continuing my journey home. After ten minutes or so, I'm aware of a brightness in the car and I look in the rear view mirror to see if I should pull over and let someone overtake. There's nothing to see, yet the inside of the car is lit in a bluey white glow. I sometimes wonder if I might witness some sort of UFO landing on this stretch of road, with no fellow humans to corroborate my story. After a few tricky attempts to squint out of all windows while driving I see it's not aliens at all, it's still just me, and the moon glowing through the break in the clouds.

For a finite period I am spatially, geographically and psychologically remote.

A NOTE ON REMOTENESS
Bram Thomas Arnold

Written on the autumn equinox, 2014, Cornwall.

I am typing this in a small valley, three miles from the most Southerly tip of mainland England. And yet, I have also just read an extract from Ed Miliband's speech to the Labour conference in Manchester, received an update on the US bombings of ISIS strongholds in Raqqa, Syria, as well as purchasing a copy of *Hyperobjects* by Timothy Morton. In short I have procrastinated my way through a good 45 minutes of precious time, that until recently in this house, I would have spent writing by hand in my notebook.

Contemporary remoteness is exposed by digital isolation, the proliferation of the off-grid retreat, the desperate attempts at attaining mobile signal, waving our phones in the air as we stand on tree-stumps in fields, or the enthusiasm with which one celebrates one's imminent off-gridness online – 'I can't wait! Five weeks of no internet, no phones at an Ayurvedic retreat, see you all in November …'.

I can also, however, remember a time (pre-mobile phones), in which I would step out of my front door in a city and luxuriate in the immediate remoteness one can feel when you realise that no one you know has any idea where you are right now. I used to walk the streets of Wellington in New Zealand in 2004 fuelled by this glorious sense of remoteness and isolation.

Remoteness these days can perhaps be accomplished by switching off the devices: those wireless boxes that have invaded our homes with their perpetual blinks and winks, abandoning your clever phone, your tablet and your laptop and your computer; it's a lot to give I know. I grew up as one of a generation that was told that if everyone turned their TV's off standby we'd be able to close four whole power stations. Instead of doing this we invented a whole new form of technology that doesn't even come with the option of leaving it on standby. They are all just perpetually on, whirring away into the night, helping us download the latest illegal episode of whatever.

Remoteness, like Nature, has assumed an affiliation with the 'Great Outdoors', with wilderness, and wildness, the wild places. Yet whilst in Scotland, preparing for *Remote Performances* by wild-camping on the north face of An Gearanach facing Ben Nevis, I was still able to receive a text from a friend 656 miles away on the shores of the south coast of England, asking me when I'd be home.

Turn the damn things off. Step outside. Immediate remoteness is achieved. Half way up a hillside with a satellite and a bunch of technical wizards from London we were together alone at *Outlandia*, perpetually tweeting our excitement at all this space and all this time, to just be, existing in a perpetual state of contradiction. Anytime I received an unexpected txt or alert it made me wish I had forgotten my charger.

Fig. 46 (above)   *Outlandia* with satellite dish, August 2014
Source: Inga Tillere
Fig. 47 (below)   View from *Outlandia*, Glen Nevis, August 2014
Source: Inga Tillere

ENDNOTES ON REMOTENESS 155

Fig. 48 (above)   *Outlandia*, August 2014
Source: Inga Tillere

Fig. 49 (below)   Tam Dean Burn, Loch Ailort Inn, August 2014
Source: Inga Tillere

Fig. 50 (above)　Johny Brown and James Stephen Finn, Tradewinds, Corpach, August 2014
Source: Inga Tillere

Fig. 51 (below)　Left to right: Benedict Drew, Lee Patterson, Bruce Gilchrist, Tam Dean Burn, Johny Brown, James Stephen Finn, Corpach, August 2014
Source: Inga Tillere

Further Resources

Further details of *Outlandia* and *Remote Performances* are online at:

Outlandia http://www.outlandia.com
Remote Performances http://www.remoteperformances.co.uk

In addition to resources referenced in the individual pieces of writing, the following may be of interest:

BOOKS

Bachelard, Gaston (1994) *The Poetics of Space*. Boston: Beacon Press.

Deakin, Roger (2000) *Waterlog*. London: Vintage.

Evans, David (2013) *The Art of Walking*. London: Black Dog.

Harmon, Katherine (2003) *You Are Here: Personal Geographies and Other Maps of the Imagination*. New York: Princeton Architectural Press.

Hodge, Stephen; Persighetti, Simon; Smith, Phil; Turner, Cathy and Weaver, Tony (2006) *A Mis-Guide to Anywhere*. Exeter: Wrights & Sites.

Kastner, Jeff (1998) *Land and Environmental Art*. London: Phaidon.

Lane, Cathy and Carlyle, Angus, eds. (2013) *In the Field*. Axminster: Uniform Books.

Latour, Bruno (1993) *We Have Never Been Modern*. Cambridge, Mass: Harvard University Press.

Macfarlane, Robert (2008) *Mountains of the Mind: A History of a Fascination*. London: Granta.

Macfarlane, Robert (2013) *The Old Ways*. London: Penguin.

Marsching, Jane and Polli, Andrea (2012) *Far Field: Digital Culture, Climate Change, and the Poles*. Bristol: Intellect.

Massey, Doreen (2005) *For Space*. Gateshead: Sage.

Morrison-Bell, Cynthia (2013) *Walk On: From Richard Long to Janet Cardiff 40 Years of Art Walking*. Sunderland: Art Editions North.

Muir, John (2009) *Journeys in the Wilderness*. Edinburgh: Birlinn.

O'Rourke, Karen (2013) *Walking and Mapping: Artists as Cartographers*. Cambridge, Mass.: MIT Press.

Perec, Georges (2008) *Species of Spaces and Other Pieces*. London: Penguin.

Solnit, Rebecca (2006) *A Field Guide to Getting Lost*. London: Canongate Books.

Solnit, Rebecca (2001) *Wanderlust: A History of Walking*. London: Verso.

JOURNAL ARTICLES

(2012) 'On Foot', *Performance Research*, 17: 2.

Heddon, Dee and Turner, Cathy (2010) 'Walking Women: Interviews with Artists on the Move', *Performance Research*, 15: 4, pp. 14–22.

Milliard, Coline (2010) 'Walks of Life', *Art Monthly*, 337, 6 October, pp. 1–4.

Warr, Tracey (2002) 'Circuitry', *Performance Research*, 6: 3, pp. 8–12.

Wilkie, Fiona (2012) 'Site-specific Performance and the Mobility Turn', *Contemporary Theatre Review*, 22: 02, pp. 203–12.

Williams, David (2010) 'Underworld, Underground, Underhistory: Towards a Counterhistory of Waste and Wasteland', *Performance Research*, 15: 4, pp. 131–40.

ARTISTS' REMOTE RESIDENCIES AND OTHER WEBSITES OF INTEREST

Atlas http://atlasarts.org.uk

Canal and River Trust Arts on the Waterways https://canalrivertrust.org.uk/art-and-the-canal-and-river- trust/arts-on-the-waterways-2014

Centre d'Art i Natura, Farrera http://www.farreracan.cat

Cove Park http://covepark.org

Deveron Arts http://www.deveron-arts.com

Frontiers in Retreat http://frontiersinretreat.org

Mustarinda http://www.mustarinda.fi

Nevis Partnership http://www.nevislandscape.co.uk

NIDA Art Colony http://www.nidacolony.lt

Resartis http://www.resartis.org

River Tamar Project http://tamarproject.org.uk

Scottish Sculpture Workshop http://www.ssw.org.uk

Skaftfell http://skaftfell.is/en/skaftfell/

Timespan http://timespan.org.uk

Transartists http://www.transartists.org

Urbonas, Nomeda and Gediminas, *Uto-pia* http://www.vilma.cc/uto-pia

Wysing Arts Centre http://www.wysingartscentre.org

Index

Illustrations are shown in **bold**.

adaptation 56–7, 62
Anderson, Willie **Plate xviii**
Anthropocene 47, 49, 52–3, 87
architecture xvii, 1–9, 12, 46, 59, 86; *see also* huts; hutopia; inhabit
archive xiv, xvii, 45, 50, 58–9; *see also* taxonomy
Arisaig Highland Games **37**, 41
Arnold, Bram Thomas xiii, 49, 105–11, 153
   Reading Particle Physics to a River 49, **108**
   Reading Poetry to a Rock 49, **109**
   Swearing An Oath to a Scottish Glen 49, **Plate xxix**
   Throwing Rocks at Trees 49, **107**
art 2, 6–7, 44, 50–51, 141–50, 151
   and ecology xiii, xv, xvii, xix, 2, 16, 45, 50–52, 59, 83–90, 105–11
   and fieldwork xix, 6, 15–20, 37–41, 50, 69–72, **73**, 73–5, **77**, **83**, 83–90, 93, 101–4, 137–8, **Plate xxv**, **Plate xxxiii**
   and geography 16, 50, 52, **80**, 115, 125, 151
   and history xiv, xix, 2, 9, 12, 14, 16, 18, 45, 48, 52, 57–8, 65, 68, 93, 157–8
   and maps xiv, **6,** 12, 49–52, 59, 66, 74, 115, 125, 133, 152, 157–8
   and physics 13–14, 49, 51, 56, 107
   and research 51, 57, 149
   and science xvii, xix, xx, 14, 87, 89, 92

art making 9, 13, 49–51, 96
   and collaboration xv, xvii, xix, 7, 13, 30–31, 37–41, 69–72, 86, 102, 150
   and materials 5, 55–62
   and place xvii, xviii, 7, 9, 11–14, 17, 19, 43–53, 57, 63–8, 69–72, 83–90, 102, 104, 113–27, 136, 142, 151–3
art residencies xv, xx, 6, 30, 46, 50, 53, 60, 158
Atlas Arts 158, **Plate xix**

bagpipes 38–9
Band of Holy Joy xiv, **Plate xxxvii**, **Plate xl**; *see also* Johny Brown
Barker, Ruth xiii-xiv, 50–51, **113**, 113–27, **Plate xxxiv**
Baxter, Ed xiv, 6, 49–51, 91–9
Ben Nevis 2, 4, **11**, 12–13, 16, 19, 38, 40–41, 45–6, 51, 56, 74, 96, 131, 136, 153, 158
birds xix, 16, 19, 38–40, 46, 51, 55–62, 84, 110, 137, 152
Brisley, Stuart 149–50
   Untitled landscape (verso) **Plate xxxviii**
   Untitled landscape (recto) **Plate xxxix**
Brown, Johny xiv 6–7, 49–51, **129**, 129–40, **156**
   Into Outlandia **Plate xxxvii**, **Plate xl**
   and see Band of Holy Joy
Burn, Tam Dean xiv, 6–7, **91**, 92–3, **155**, **156**
Calvino, Italo 49, 52
Campbell, Isabel 41, **Plate xv**
cartography, *see* art and maps

Cèilidh Trailers 39, 46, **Plate xiv**
childhood 2, 16, 20, 46, 66, 93, 96, 107
Chinnery, Clair xiv–xv, 48, 51, 55–62, 151
   The Boatswain's Call **55, Plate xxviii**
   Briefe and True: Lost Landscapes 56–7,
     62
   Cuculus Prospectus xiv, 56–61
   Existing New World Servants 59
   Generic Highland Hybrid Host 1 59,
     Plate xxvi
   Generic Highland Hybrid Host 2 59, **60,**
     61, Plate xxvii
   How to Speak …: The Breeding Birds of
     the United Kingdom 56
   The Human Nest-Box 56–61
Clark, Norman 5, 31
Clearings 45
climate change xx, 47, 49, 52–3, 57, 157
climbing 2, 5, 13–14, 47
coast 17, 30, 47, 57, 61, 64, 117, 123, 146,
   153
Cockburn, Ken xv, 31, 50 **Plate xxxv**
  The Road North 31
colonisation xiv, 48, 53, 55–62, 107
composition xvi, xix, 69–72, 73–5, 51,
   92
computer music xvi, 34
contemporary remote 48, 51, 53, 83–90,
   152–3; *see also* remoteness
Creagh Dubh Mountaineering Club
   12–13
Crosby, Alfred W. 57, 61–2

Dant, Adam 6–7
  A Journey Through the Great Glen to the
    Library of Outlandia **6**
  Bibliotheque Outlandia **7**
Davidson Kelly, Kirsteen xv, 51, 69–72
distillery 39, 41, 46
drawing xiii, xviii, **3**, 56, 64, 142–4, 147–8,
   149
Drew, Benedict xv, 48, 77–81, **156**
  Notes for a Video **Plates i–iv**
Du Toit, Alex 45, 52

ecology, *see* art and ecology
Edinburgh Art Festival xvii, 9

environment xx, 2, 5, 7, 13–14, 36, 52, 57,
   59, 85, 87, 89, 109–11, 157
exploration 47, 51, 66
extinction 58, 62

farming 13, 39, 45, 93, 144–5, 147
field recording, *see* art and fieldwork
fieldwork, *see* art and fieldwork
Finlay, Alec xv–xvi, 25–31, 46, 50, **Plate xxxv**
  The Bothy Project xv, **26, 30**
  Circle Poem (for Outlandia) **25**
  The Road North xv–xvi, 31, 50
Finn, James Stephen **156**
flora xviii, 17, 22–3, 30, 57, 62, 64, 84, 106,
   114, 116–7, 123, 126, 151
forest xiii, xviii, 2, 5, 12, 16, 26, 38,
   45–6, 50–51, 56, 59, 63–8, 71–2, 87,
   96–9, 115, 118, 122, 125, 135–6, 138,
   142–3, 146, 148–9, **Plate xx**
Forestry Commission Scotland 5
Fort William 2, 12, 14, 22, 34, 41, 44–5, 47,
   50–51, 74, 130, **Plate xxiii**
Fraser, Malcolm 2, **3**, 5, 9, 31, 40–41
Fraser Darling, Frank 19–20, 49
future xvi, xx, 22, 48, 50, 52–3, 59, 87,
   89–90

Gaelic 7, 12, 38, 137, 139
geography, *see* art and geography
geology 17, 20, 38, 45, 47, 51, 87, 90; *see*
   also Anthropocene
Gibson, Mel **79**
Gilchrist, Bruce xvi, xvii, 7, 9, 13–14, 74,
   83–90, **156**, **Plate xxxiii**; *see also*
   London Fieldworks
Gilchrist, Jetson Joelson 41, 93
Gillespie, Alex **Plate xvii**
Glen Nevis 2, 4, 9, 12–13, 16, 40, 44–5,
   48–51, 64–5, **69**, 70, **71**, **72**, **73**, 74,
   92, **95**, **105**, 107–8, **108**, **109**, 151,
   154
  and farming, *see* farming
  and industry 2, 12–13, 48–9, 84,
   107
Goodiepal xvi, **33**, 33–6, 46, 51
  A Message to the International Hacker
   Community **35, Plates xxx–xxxi**

El Camino Del Hardcore – Rejsen Til Nordens Indre xvi, 34, 36
Greenland xvi, **83**, 83–90

habitat xvii, 56–7
Harriot, Thomas 57, 62
Harrison, M. John 13–14
Henderson, Ingrid 41, 46, **Plates xii–xiii**
Hutchison, John **Plate xvi**
hutopia 28, 31; *see also* architecture; huts; utopia
huts 25–31, 46, 50, 56, 59, 71, 86, 136–7,142–3, 148, 152; *see also* architecture; hutopia

Identity 18–19, 56, 89
inhabit 45, 47–8, 50, 56–9, 62, 64, 144, 151; *see* also architecture; huts
Iorwerth, Miriam 70–72, **71**, 92
Ireland, John **Plate xx**
islands 18–20, 47, 50, 85–7, 106, 110, 143, 147–8, **Plate xix**
Isle of Eigg xv, **26**, 30, 103

Jacobite 12, 45
The Jacobite (train) 41, 46
Jacobson, Niall **3**
Joelson, Jo xvi–xvii, 1–9, 13–14, 44, 85, 90; *see also* London Fieldworks
John Muir 158
John Muir Trust **Plate xvi**

Kenchington, Sarah xvi–xvii, 49, 51, **101**, 101–04, **103**, **Plates xxiv–xxv**

LADA, *see* Live Art Development Agency
Lanceley, Peter xiv, 6, **9**, 64, 92–3, **94**, **Plate xxi**
Land Art 48, 50
landscape xv, xvii, xviii, xix, 2, 9, 12–14, 16, 18, 46, 50–51, 56, 64–6, 71–2, 74, 84, 93, 96, 98, 106, 118, 120–122, 136, 151
language 13, 22–3, 56, 86, 95, 106, 146
listening xviii, xix, 7, 17–18, 36, 51, 137, 144–8
Live Art Development Agency xx, 6–7, 53

local xviii, xix, 2, 5–7, 44–6, 50–52, 65, 70, 74, 86–7, 92–3, 130–131, 133, 144
Local Spot broadcasts 7, 45, 52, **Plates xiii–xx**
Loch Ailort 38, 41, **43**, 49, 74, **101**, 102, **103**, **155**, **Plate xxxiii**; *see also* Roshven
Lochaber Archive Centre 45, 50
Lochaber College 5, 70
London Fieldworks xvii, xx, 2, 7, 9, 13–14, 31, 53, 83–90
    Little Earth 2, 9, 13–14
    Outlandia 1–9, 12–14, 16, 19, 25, 29, 31, 35, 44, 46, 48, 50, 53, 56, 59–60, 65–6, 71–2, 74–5, 86, 92–3, 102, **113**, 129–40, 149, 153, **154**, **155**, 157, **Plates v–xi**
    Polaria xx, **83**, 85, 90
    The Sound of Lochaber (with Mark Vernon) 7, 13, **37,** 37–41, 46; *see also* Mark Vernon
    Syzygy xx, 85–6, 90

McColl, Ian 45, **Plate xv**
Macfarlane, Robert 13–14, 46–7, 52, 68, 157
McKee, Francis xvii–xviii, 11–14
maps, *see* art and maps
Menzies, Charlie 70–72, **72**, 92
midge 16, 46, 134, 138
migration xiv, 56–7, 62, 84, 152
Morton, Timothy 48, 52, 85, 90, 106, 110–111, 153
mountain xv–xvi, 2, 5, 12–13, 16–18, 20, 30–1, 39–40, 46–7, 70, 74, **78**, 86, 92, 96, 102, 107–8, 110, 114–5, 120–121, 125–6, 131, 135, 157; *see also* Ben Nevis
mountaineering, *see* climbers; mountain

Nature xiv, xvii, xix, 30, 38, 44, 46–52, 64, 68, **Plates i–iv**, 84, 87, 89–90, 93, 96–8, 106, 108–11, 135, 153
Nevis Landscape Partnership, *see* Ben Nevis
Nicholson, Emma **Plate xix**

Nicol, Sarah 6, 92–3, **Plate xx**
O'Brien, Lisa xviii, **63**, 63–8, 152–3,
   Plate xxi
  Balgy Panorama left **65**
  Torridon Forest, January **67**
off-grid 2, 7, 13, 44, 46–7, 86, 153
Outlandia, see London Fieldworks

Patterson, Lee xviii, 48–9, 51, **73**, 73–5,
   137, **156**, **Plates xxxii–xxxiii**
Pedersen, Michael xviii–xix, 21–3, 50–51
  Like Like 22–3
performances 7, 9, 16, 19, 45, 49–50, 61,
   70, 72, 86, 96, **105**, **108**, **109**, 130,
   149, 158; *see also* performative
performative 9, 60, 86; *see also*
   performances
place, *see* art making and place
plants, *see* flora

radio xiv, xviii, xix, 6–7, 16, 34–5, 41,
   44–5, 49–50, 52, 75, 85–7, 89, 92–3,
   95–6, 136, 140, 144, 146, 148, 149,
   152, **Plates xxxiv–xxxvii**
Remote Performances 6, 9, 13, **15**, 16, 18,
   33, 34, 41, 44–5, 49–53, 56, 61–2,
   63, 70, 74, 86, 92–3, 96, **105**, **108**,
   109, **129**, **141**, 149, 151, 153, 157,
   Plates xxi–xxxvii, xl; *and see Remote
   Performances* LADA Blog Posts;
   Remote Performances Tumblr
Remote Performances LADA Blog Posts 7,
   9, 53
Remote Performances Tumblr 157
Remoteness xviii, xx, 9, 17, 19, 36,
   44, 46–8, 51–3, 56–9, 61–2, 64–8,
   74, 84–7, 89, 94, 102–4, 136, 149,
   151–3, 157–8; *see also* contemporary
   remote; *Study Room Guide to
   Remoteness*
Resonance 104.4fm xiv, xviii, xix, 6–7,
   34–5, 44, 74, 86
Resonance Radio Orchestra 92, **Plate xxxvi**
rivers 16, 18–19, 23, 47–8, 51, 70, **108**,
   115, 125, 152, 158
Romanticism xiii, 18, 48, 93–4, 96,
   108–10, 135

Roshven 41, 47, 74, **77**; *see also* Loch
   Ailort
rural 2, 7, 41, 47–8, 87, 106, 138, 149

Sacramento, Nuno 51, 53
Sample, Geoff xix, **15**, 15–20, 48–9, 51,
   137
Scotland xv, xvi, xvii–xviii, 13, 18, 20, 27,
   50, 64, 130, 137, 145, 147, 153; *see
   also* Scottish
  and the Acts of Union 18
  and independence 18, 151
Scottish 12–14, 16–19, 45, 47, 84, 107,
   130, 139, 151, 158
  and Enlightenment 6
sea 47, 49, 51, 53, 89, 101–4, 147,
   Plate xxxiii; *see also* coast
seasons 17, 22, 46, 48, 65
shepherd 45, 96, **Plate xv**
Smithson, Robert 14, 45, 52, **80**
Solnit, Rebecca 48, 52, 158
sound art xiv, xvi, xvii, xviii, xix, xx, 2, 7, 9,
   13, 16–18, 34, 38–9, 41, 44–6, 48–52,
   56, 61, 64, 66, 85, 92, 94–6, 102–3,
   114–9, 122–6, 133, 136–7, 140, 144,
   146
storytelling xviii, 50–53
Study Room Guide to Remoteness xx, 53
sublime 14, 18

taxonomy 56–8; *see also* archive
technology xvii, 7, **8**, 9, 34–6, 44–5, 47,
   49, 74–5, 85–7, 90, 153, **154**
territory 44, 57, 85
time 22–3, 34–6, 45, 48–52, 66–7, 71,
   74, 84, 90, 92–3, 96–7, 114–7, 123–6,
   134, 138–9, 149, 153
topography 51, 115, 125
tourism 2, 5, 12, 22, 45, 64–5, 74, **81**
treehouse 12, 46, 66, 86
Turchi, Peter 50–52

Umney, Michael 6, 92
urban 36, 46, 48, 51, 56, 84, 86–7,
   138
utopia 13, 48; *see also* hutopia 28, 31
Vernon, Mark xix, **Plates xxii–xxiii**

The Sound of Lochaber (with London Fieldworks) 7, 13, **37**, 37–41, 46

walking xiii, 5, 23, 38, 50–52, 64–6, 70, 97, 108, 110, 115, 118, 122, 138, 157–8; *see also* Walking Stewart
Walking Stewart 93–4, 96–7
Warr, Tracey xix–xx, 6, 43–53, 158
 and Writers' Workshop 50–51, 53
weather xviii, 16, 18, 22, 45–6, 51, 64–5, 85–6, 140
White, Tony xx, 19, 49, **141**

'High-Lands' 141–50
'Stormbringer' 19, 50
wild xvi, xix, 2, 9, 12–14, 16, 19, 26–7, 36, 45, 47, 51–2, 64–8, 70, **78**, **81**, 84, 87, 90, 106–7, 114, 116–8, 122–4, 126, 138–9, 153, 158, **Plate i**
wilderness, *see* wild
wildlife xix, 2, 15–20, 44, 67, 84, 139; *see also* birds
Wilson, C.T.R. 2, 13,
Wilson, E.O. 47, 53
woods, *see* forest